Secrets
OF YOUR
Rising Sign

ABOUT THE AUTHOR

Andrea Taylor (Dorset, England) has been an astrological counselor for over forty years. Originally self-taught, she studied through the Huber School in the mid-1980s. She started teaching birth chart interpretation soon after, and she's had clients worldwide. Andrea also authored *The Astrology Book* and *Birth Chart Interpretation Plain & Simple*.

ANDREA TAYLOR

Secrets OF YOUR Rising Sign

Discover Your Past and True Self

Llewellyn Publications | Woodbury, Minnesota

FIRST EDITION
First Printing, 2024

Book design by Samantha Peterson
Cover design by Kevin R. Brown

Llewellyn Publications is a registered trademark of Llewellyn Worldwide Ltd.

Library of Congress Cataloging-in-Publication Data
Names: Taylor, Andrea, author.
Title: Secrets of your rising sign : discover your past and true self / by
    Andrea Taylor.
Description: First edition. | Woodbury, MN : Llewellyn Publications, a
    division of Llewellyn Worldwide Ltd., 2024. | Summary: "This book
    explores each rising sign, its significance in your natal chart, and how
    it's connected to the south node, which is a common past-life marker"
    —Provided by publisher.
Identifiers: LCCN 2024003208 (print) | LCCN 2024003209 (ebook) | ISBN
    9780738776675 | ISBN 9780738776712 (ebook)
Subjects: LCSH: Zodiac. | Birth charts. | Astrology.
Classification: LCC BF1726 .T39 2024 (print) | LCC BF1726 (ebook) | DDC
    133.5/2—dc23/eng/20240226
LC record available at https://lccn.loc.gov/2024003208
LC ebook record available at https://lccn.loc.gov/2024003209

Llewellyn Publications
A Division of Llewellyn Worldwide Ltd.
2143 Wooddale Drive
Woodbury, MN 55125-2989
www.llewellyn.com

Printed in the United States of America

OTHER BOOKS BY ANDREA TAYLOR

The Astrology Book

Birth Chart Interpretation Plain & Simple

What's Your Big Three?

For Alexandra, my wonderful daughter, who is an amazing mother, teacher, friend, and life-giver (via surrogacy) to others. May the universe return the blessings she so freely gives.

Man's main concern is not to gain pleasure or to avoid pain but rather to see a meaning in his life.

—Viktor E. Frankl,
Man's Search for Meaning

Contents

CHAPTER TWO: THE NODES AND THE HOUSES — 87

CHAPTER THREE: THE NODES AND THE SIGNS — 165

CHAPTER FOUR: COMBINING THE NODES AND THE SIGNS — 209

Introduction

For eons, our ancestors gazed at the stars and wondered why they were here and what their purpose was. Perhaps you wonder too. For thousands of years, the tool to answer these questions was out of ordinary people's reach, yet astrology has been around almost as long as the human race. Now, we know to turn to our astrological birth chart for answers.

Prior to the twentieth century, a birth chart was used to answer the most basic questions—chart interpretation was all about prediction. *Where is my son? Will this ship make port? Will I marry well? When will I die?* These were the questions on people's lips. A birth chart can answer these questions—and these sorts of questions do remain, of course—but they have been superseded by our more complex needs. Nowadays, many of us are seeking answers to our life's purpose, as well as guidance on how to lead a fulfilling life.

As the human race has grown in wisdom and understanding, so too has astrologers' comprehension of birth charts. We now realize a birth chart is multifaceted and multilayered, and that it's possible to use a chart to unveil mysteries and gain further enlightenment. There are psychological elements of a birth chart that were not even considered by our astrological forebears, but were there to find by those who chose to expand their mental horizons.

Now, many people believe we have more than one lifetime for our souls to spiritually evolve and grow. This book will explain how, in my view, your birth chart shows not only who you were and how you lived in your last life, it also provides an answer to these two elusive questions: Why are you here now? And what is your purpose in this lifetime?

Someone once said to me that everything we need is around us—all we require is the wisdom to see it. This is so true! There is no end to the secrets a birth chart can reveal, *but we have to ask the right questions.* After forty years of interpreting birth charts, I've realized an individual's chart provides everything they need for this life's journey, and there are three areas of a chart that hold these answers: the rising sign and the north and south nodes.

The south nodes have been an accepted past-life marker since the last century. I will go into more depth later on. Additionally, based on my years of experience, I believe that *the rising sign is also a past-life marker*, and in the following chapters I will explain why I believe that and how you can use your rising sign to discover your own life path.

The great thing is, to access this information, you don't have to know all about your birth chart, or even know much about astrology! These methods are accessible even if you know nothing about astrology. Once you realize how significant your birth chart is, you'll likely be motivated to learn more about it. In the meantime, there is a chapter at the end of this book that provides some basic astrological information. If you do want to learn more about your birth chart and all of the energies you were given to help you on your journey, check out my book *Birth Chart Interpretation Plain & Simple*. It's for complete beginners and gently leads you through your own chart interpretation, and you can go on to interpret others' charts too. Another book of mine, *What's Your Big Three?*, takes an in-depth look at how your sun, moon, and rising signs reveal who you really are.

CREATING YOUR BIRTH CHART

If you aren't familiar with your own birth chart, there are lots of sites that will create your birth chart for you for free. These sites will ask for your time, date, and place of birth. Without a precise time of birth, you cannot be sure your chart is accurate. Our planet is moving all the time—it orbits the sun, but also revolves as it does so—so rising signs shift every two hours or so. (Your rising sign is the astrological sign that was rising on the eastern horizon when you were born.)

The time of your birth is incredibly important—if your rising sign is miscalculated, your entire chart will be affected. If you do not know your time of birth, check your birth certificate. If your time of birth is not listed, or if you don't have access to this document, try to find out from other family members if they recall anything about the day you were born so you can at least take an educated guess.

Once you have created your chart, determine your rising sign. Rising signs are always on the far left of the birth chart. The rising sign used to be called the Ascendant, and it is still abbreviated on most charts as AC—though, just to confuse matters, it is often written as *As* in the planet list that's provided with most birth charts. If you can't find AC on the chart, look for As in the planet list, and that's your rising sign.

Then, find your north node. The north node symbol looks like a headset or a horseshoe, and it's always the last thing on the list of planets. Make a note of the astrological sign it's in, and also jot down the house, as the nodes are always interpreted using both. The south nodes typically do not appear on a birth chart but are exactly opposite the north node. For example, if the north node is at 20 degrees Aries, the south node will be in Libra at 20 degrees.

For those who aren't familiar with astrology and who want to learn more, there is an appendix at the back of the book that provides some basic information. This will help familiarize you with the astrological terms mentioned in the book.

WHAT BIRTH CHARTS CAN TEACH US ABOUT THE RISING SIGN

The rising sign is the most elusive concept of the whole chart. Even some experienced astrologers find it hard to explain. When I was learning astrology, my teachers believed that we gradually become our rising sign as our life progresses, a theory that was quickly debunked by my own experience interpreting charts. It was obvious we already have a very good grasp of how to use our rising sign. The general consensus among astrologers these days is that the rising sign is a protection, a buffer zone between us and the outside world, a doorway through which we must pass each time we interact with people.

Imagine the birth chart circle as you, and everything outside of that circle as the outside world (everyone and everything else), with the rising sign as the doorway. Each and every time you have contact with the outside world, you unconsciously filter what you say and do through this doorway of the first house, and everything others say and do must pass through this doorway as well. The astrological sign that sits in the doorway colours all you do and all you say. It's like putting on a coat before going outside: you feel safe and comfortable wearing it when leaving your inner sanctuary and joining the outside world.

While this concept made sense to me, two questions remained: Why do we need this buffer between us and the outside world? And how do we have such a clear knowledge of our rising sign? Even people who do not know the slightest thing about astrology embody their rising sign, and it has been clear since the moment of birth! If we have a Cancer rising sign, we cried a lot as infants; if we have a Leo rising, we demanded attention; if Scorpio, we were good babies because we hate showing our needs; if Taurus, we were easily placated by food and warmth; and so on. These questions and realisations led me to deeper exploration, and I now believe *the rising sign has a far deeper significance* than previously realized.

My belief is that we do live more than one life so our souls can develop and learn, but that each time we are born, we enter into a new world, with a new path to follow and new lessons to learn, so our birth chart is completely new too. But the universe is supportive, not unkind, and thus we are not sent into this current existence without protection. We carry with us safety blankets from our previous life: we have our "home" to retreat to, our south node (more about that in chapter 2), and we have our rising sign, our protective layer. And the *rising sign, I believe, was our sun sign in the last life.*

This is a new theory, but it explains *why* we have such a detailed knowledge of our rising sign characteristics from the moment we are born. It explains why we use the rising sign as we do, why we so readily and comfortably hide our true selves behind the familiar aspects of our rising sign. Why else would we adopt the characteristics of a sign that very often doesn't even have a planet in it? Nowhere else in our charts do we use an astrological sign that does not have a planet in it! A planet draws our attention and focus to an area, but the houses (areas of life) without a planet (sometimes called empty houses) hold little interest. Although some people do have planets in their first house, many more don't; even so, they embody their rising sign just the same.

Our rising sign is so instantly adopted and used that I believe it has to be a past life memory/experience, and that it is there to provide us with safety and security in this brand new, amazing world. It gives us the confidence to start again, to begin anew. We assume our familiar rising sign characteristics while finding our way with the planet combinations and energies in our current birth chart, which are there to assist us in confronting the challenges of this lifetime. This theory also explains why we actually need a rising sign as a buffer. It becomes obvious it is a necessary protection against the outside world, which is overflowing with available knowledge and wisdom, as well as rubbish and distraction. Our rising sign guides our interactions with the outside world so that we don't lose who we are.

In our digital age, where communication is freely available in so many forms, this buffer is more relevant than ever. Our world is awash with mindless, senseless chatter and many false pathways; it is full of people all vying for our attention. It is so easy to get drawn into the outside world—it is entertaining, and it distracts us. But most of it is completely useless for our own spiritual growth. All the outside world does is perpetuate our blindness to reality: the reality of our world, and our true lessons.

How many people have you seen walking outside yet plugged into their phone, either listening to music or a podcast, or texting or calling someone? We are constantly being drawn away from our reality into what the outside world has created. The problem, as I see it, is finding our way through all of this to our own soul's purpose. Only when we understand what we are supposed to be learning in this life can we be selective about what we accept into our self through the doorway of our rising sign.

We are taught that true spiritual enlightenment comes when we let go of our ego, when we do things because they feel right and resonate within us, and not in order to gain any outward praise, recognition, or reward. This, then, is the path to aim for through your rising sign if you want to use it at its highest vibration.

The first chapter of this book aims to guide you through the twelve rising signs and the spiritual development and wisdom required by each. It also explains how to fully use your own rising sign in its most effective way in order to fulfil your soul's purpose.

And how do you know your soul's purpose? Via the nodes. The nodes have long been seen as cosmic points that show us where we have come from (the south node) as well as where we are headed (the north node). Very often, there is no planet in the south node sign or house, yet, like the rising sign, the south node area is one we are familiar with and comfortable in. In chapters 2 and 3, we will look at the nodes and what part they play in our spiritual journey.

one
Secrets of the Twelve Rising Signs

So, by now you know why you have a rising sign: it was your sun sign in the last life, which makes it natural and easy to assume these characteristics now.

In this lifetime, our rising sign has two roles: it gives us a feeling of safety in our initial interactions with others while we assess their intentions and determine whether or not we want further communication with them, and it shows us what to filter from the outside world, and how.

Because each of our lifetimes has a unique birth chart, our familiar rising sign allows us to adapt to our new arrangement of planets and energies that will give us the necessary focus to fulfil this life's lessons.

Each rising sign has a special spiritual lesson. If your sun sign is not the same as your rising sign, you succeeded in learning its lessons in the last life. If your sun sign is the same as your rising sign this time, these lessons were not fully absorbed in the last life, so you cannot move on to another sun sign.

Very often, people with the same sun and rising sign become famous. It is impossible to hide a first-house sun because the first house is on display; people immediately see any planets there. And, as the sun is so powerful, its energies cannot be contained. This means your actions will be held up to the light and judged by many, so it behoves you to act in accordance with the sun's highest spiritual energies, and to use this placement wisely. The descriptions in this chapter can guide you towards how to express your sun the right way if it's in your rising sign.

Finally—and this bears repeating, because it is incredibly important—never forget that the birth chart circle is you. It is your life map. It shows where you come from and where you are going, and the lessons you are learning in this life. Everything outside of this chart circle is the outside world, which, quite frankly, doesn't care whether you are evolving or not. You will be bombarded with unnecessary dross as you live your life, from fashion fads to endless chatter about nothing, and you will be led down many false avenues. Commercialism is rife—it underpins our whole world—so it is a challenge to interact with the outside world without losing your sense of self. But, if you are grounded in your rising sign and sure of your path and your lessons in this life, as shown by your north node, you won't be swayed by these external forces. You will stay true to you.

The following descriptions of the rising signs explain their characteristics as well as their unique spiritual lesson. Each rising sign has the possibility of reaching its highest vibration, but also its lowest. At each and every step of life, you get to make that choice, but you can't choose wisely if you don't understand your rising sign.

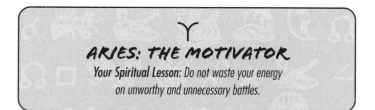

♈ ARIES: THE MOTIVATOR

Your Spiritual Lesson: Do not waste your energy on unworthy and unnecessary battles.

Because Aries rules the first house and its planet is warlike Mars, they are fast, forceful, me-minded, proactive leaders and so rarely pass through life unnoticed. Because this was your sun sign in the last life, you feel at home using the sign of Aries as a safety blanket and a disguise separating you and the outside world

Everyone who knows you will be aware of your opinions and actions because Aries is a cardinal fire sign, and as such, you are not afraid to stand up for what you believe in, to face confrontation, or to march into battle. Whether it is arguing with a bad driver, asserting your rights, sharing your ideas with others, or playing a competitive sport, no one will doubt that you are independent and decisive, bold and brave. No obstacle stops you once you have made a decision, and your decisions are very quick—immediate, in fact. You base your actions on gut instinct, and if something appeals, you don't second-guess yourself. Your symbol is the ram, which shows your head-down determination to get your way, and to go your own way. Rams don't pussyfoot around—they charge right up to an obstacle and batter it down with brute force.

In your last life, you inhabited these characteristics for so long that they feel incredibly comfortable now, which is why you've adopted them as a defence against the world.

In your last life, you would have lived independently. That does not necessarily mean you had no partnerships, but you probably shouldered the responsibility of others and took charge. Because of this, you found it hard to compromise and fit in with others in your personal relationships. This would have meant you either lived alone or lived as if you *were* alone, going your own way despite appeals from your partner.

The thing you cannot tolerate from anyone is emotions—you loathe it when people get emotional. Yours is not an empathic sign, and you actively avoid pandering to others who are ill or unhappy. Nor do you like laziness in mind or body.

Each astrological sign has a purpose, and Aries' is to begin new projects, to forge new pathways, to clear the way for change and progress. That was why you were given that drive, ambition, and innocent belief that things will always work out okay, along with an undiluted idealism and faith in your own ability to cope with life and all it throws at you.

You learnt in the last life how to be bold and adventurous, how to forge ahead with your own ideas and fight for the underdog. You learnt how to do battle, whether that was actual war or verbal confrontation. You found out that being dependent on no one but yourself was great, and you liked the fact that nothing fazed you, that you didn't crumple in a heap when life didn't work out the way you'd have liked, that you had the courage and boldness to pick yourself up and start again regardless of what life threw at you. In effect, you learnt about your own personality, and you tested your strengths.

Why is it that your sign of Aries is so driven? The answer to this is threefold. Firstly, because it's a fire sign, and fire signs are full of energy and enthusiasm. Secondly, because it is a cardinal sign, which means it is proactive and likes getting things done. Finally, it is also the first sign of the zodiac, which in astrological terms is the child.

Children are very me-focused. Anyone who has had a child or been around children knows very well that they soon make a fuss if their needs aren't met. A baby can disrupt everyone's peace and harmony if it feels hungry or needs its diaper changed, and toddlers leave us in no doubt when they want something, and want it now. Children do not consider how their behaviour affects others; they just want what they want.

This is how your sign works. You want something, so you go get it. You hate listening to advice because you still want what you want, regardless of whether or not others think it's unwise. You don't actually care what they think. You want your own way. Aries is all about "me." In the last life, you learnt how to be yourself, how to get your own needs and desires met, and how to express all that fiery energy and drive.

The sign of Aries has a real task in life: to motivate others, to be the leader, to be the first into battle, to fight for the underdog, and to push for change. However, the spiritual task with Aries rising is developing the ability to distinguish important, real battles from unimportant, unnecessary ones. Your first response is always a form of aggression, because that's the way you are designed. But if you spend your life fighting everything and everyone, you are dissipating your energy and creating negative cycles.

Aries risings are meant to be strong and to fight, but your learning curve is to choose your battles because they are worth fighting for, and not to instantly react to every-thing and everyone who thwarts you. Find a cause that has meaning; find a battle that brings change and hope to others. It could be standing up as a spokesperson to block a new road that will damage the environment, or making sure underprivileged children are given equal opportu-nities. Whatever motivates you, go for it. This is the type of battle you were designed for! Always keep in mind the higher path. Save your energy for fighting real causes that have worthy outcomes. This is why you were given such energy and drive. Don't waste this energy shouting at a slow driver or trying to race faster than the car next to you.

If your sun is in Aries in this life as well, you will have nowhere to hide. The sun must express itself in this first house, so you will be an Aries through and through. You will express yourself forcefully in life. The sun is here again because you didn't fully integrate all your Aries qualities in the last life, so you are being given a second chance to learn how to direct your impressive energy into meaning-ful beginnings rather than just starting something because the opportunity presents itself. You are being given another chance to express all you are in a more focused, less ran-dom way, and to conserve your energy for worthy battles. Find a cause and focus your energy into that. No matter what else you do in life, make sure you do something that makes you proud that you pushed through change and fought for the underdog.

If your sun and rising are in Aries, your spiritual lesson is to remember that the only person you are really in competition with is yourself, so your task is to make yourself better. This lifetime is all about you, no one else. But that doesn't mean you should barge through people's sensitivities without a thought. You certainly are me-focused and you are supposed to be, but we all have to live together in harmony, so be aware of possible negative results in the way you act, and use your considerable energy and strength wisely by protecting others rather than overriding them. Your lesson is to work hard just because you can, to take action just because you can, and to lead just because you can, and for no other reason than it feels right for you.

To those of you who have a different sun sign this time around, go ahead and be who you are. Use your Aries rising sign as you become familiar with your new sun sign and your new birth chart. Keep being bold, fearless, brave, and independent. Embrace the uncomplicated, me-focused person you learned how to be so successfully. Fight for the underdog, for good causes, and for worthy reasons, and continue to do so while you learn all the lessons this life throws at you.

In order to focus your Aries energy positively, use the following list as a guide.

1. Make sure your instant reaction is not always negative.

2. Try not to take everything as a personal challenge. If someone disagrees, try to shrug rather than argue unless it really is important to stand your ground.

3. Keep in mind your energy and drive is for beginning new projects. Find a cause that inspires you, and use your strengths in a positive way by making changes that help others.

4. Avoid the "what goes around comes around" scenario by being mindful of others, and apologize if you realize you've overstepped in your enthusiasm of the moment.

5. Now and then, make an effort to hear someone out, especially your partner!

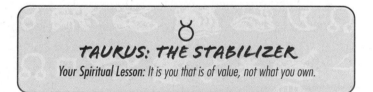

♉
TAURUS: THE STABILIZER
Your Spiritual Lesson: *It is you that is of value, not what you own.*

No matter what you have inherited by birth in this lifetime, you carry with you, as your rising sign, the past life knowledge of your previous sun sign, Taurus. This is your shield against unwanted trespasses, and you will easily but almost unconsciously display the characteristics of this sign to everyone you meet.

Taurus is a fixed earth sign. Earth signs (there are three, Virgo and Capricorn being the other two) are exactly what you'd think: earthy and stable. But your sign is also fixed, which means it is even more stable than any of the other earth signs.

Having this rising sign means you are very cautious in all you do. You would have learnt in your last life that it is best to take your time making decisions. Your experiences gave you oodles of patience and tolerance. They gave you wonderful staying power, provided you with stamina, and also imbued you with a calm assurance that people find both reassuring and frustrating—frustrating because you have brought with you into this life the reluctance to make any changes, only taking action when it is quite obvious there is absolutely no alternative. Other people feel you are stubborn when you resist change, and it may annoy them that you can miss opportunities because you prefer the status quo. Yet, they are also reassured by your behaviour because if you say something, you mean it, and if you make a promise, you keep it. You are always there for them.

Taurus is ruled by the planet Venus. Venus seeks peace and harmony, with a little luxury thrown in. Earth signs are tactile, so you need to express your love physically.

You adore hugs and affection, good food and fine wines, a comfortable home and lifestyle, and nature in all its forms. Music, too, moves you. You may play an instrument. Even if you are not a musician, music is an important part of your life. Touch, smell, and sound are all important senses for you.

Taurus finds harmony and peace via stability. To an earth sign, stability means security, and security is achieved by being financially stable and having possessions. Make no mistake, Taurus is a loving and gentle sign who wants to live in a haven of calm. But to do this requires you to build structures that you can feel secure inside, structures that can protect you from the bombardment of constant change that is modern life. You will expend any amount of energy—albeit measured energy—to create these structures, which, for you, means money in the bank and a safe place to live. It means surrounding yourself with lovely things, preferably luxuries. (If you are wealthy, this might extend to *objet d'art* or paintings by famous artists; in other words, things that will accrue in value.) But creating this structure also involves finding the right person to share it all with.

When you've finally got what you've worked for—your house, your money, and your partner—you batten down the hatches and try to ignore the world. You don't want anything to change because it would involve starting all over again. Anything that threatens that harmony and safety you've spent so much effort creating is scary, so you refuse to acknowledge it. That's why you don't like change. It is not that you are mean or uncaring. Quite the opposite! You fear change because it takes so much effort to start all over again. You hold life at bay in order to maintain your comfortable life.

Taurus rules the second house of finances, so naturally, money is a driving force. But there is a fine line between saving and becoming obsessive. Some people save for a particular item, and although you may start with that goal, once you reach your target, the idea of actually spending the money you've saved doesn't sit right with you. What if something untoward happens? Shouldn't you keep that money for that rainy day? In any case, when you look around, you see so many people who seem to have more than you. This affects your sense of self-worth because you despair that despite all your efforts, you might never achieve such riches—which, remember, equals safety in your mind.

Your relationships suffer as a result of this mindset. The fact is, you are the most loving and loyal of signs. Once you love, you love. That's it. When you make a commitment, in your eyes, it is forever. You find it almost impossible to stop loving someone even if the relationship fails or your love is not reciprocated.

Problems arise when it dawns on your partner that you view them as one of your possessions too. It is not intentional, but your continual watching can begin to feel claustrophobic. You will surround your partner with as much luxury as you can and be generous in all things, but you cannot allow the winds of freedom to blow between you. You will drop them off and pick them up and ask where they are going and who they are meeting, and when they decide they have had enough, you will hang on even more tightly. Like everything else in your life, you extended energy to acquire this most desired partner, and the idea of losing them and having to start all over again is really scary. Add to that the fact that you might have to share half your worldly goods if they leave, and panic sets in. You cling even more.

The fact is, you are who you are, and you are unlikely to change. With your rising sign in Taurus, you spent the previous life developing this stable mindset. You are designed to think of security and peace and harmony. These lovely traits of stability and a sound sense of purpose go hand-in-hand with an inability to move on even when the obvious is staring you in the face. You struggle to let people go and to think of things other than financial security. Seen in a positive light, this makes you a beacon of stability, a person of honesty and integrity. You never let someone down, never refuse to help, never forget a friend.

But nor do you grow as a person. Once you've got your stability, you stop living. When you stop living, you stop growing spiritually. So, where are you going wrong?

The problems arise because you are constantly judging your success in life on what you own and not who you are, on your possessions and not your abilities. There will always be people who have more. But by caring so much about possessions, you are stepping out of your chart circle and allowing the outside world to rule your actions.

You have so much to offer. You can tolerate a huge amount. You weather life's storms and deal with all the traumas of those you care about. Because you are a practical, sensible person, you calmly deal with any and all difficulties that life throws your way. You just keep going. A quiet life of luxury is your aim: work hard, build, make everything comfortable, then pull up the drawbridge. You build your walls and then hide behind them. Once you've achieved your desired harmony, peace, and stillness, you seek to keep hold of it so as to save repeating the process of attainment. But it is not your acquisitions that are key to your spiritual lesson—it's your sense of self-worth.

When Taurus is your rising sign, remember you have within you all the necessary tools to be of use in the world, so by all means, work hard and build your security—it's your purpose, after all! But don't lose sight of the fact that *you* have value; your value is not solely what you have worked for. Keep reminding yourself that your amazing stability, patience, and reliability are what the right people love about you, not what you own.

Centre yourself in your own abilities, and try not to become obsessed with owning for owning's sake. Ignore what other people are doing or what they have. Don't judge yourself by any other measure than your own best qualities. Other people are on different paths and have different lessons. Try and stay inside your chart circle and stop allowing the outside world to affect how you think and act. If you stay centred, your world will be richer in every sense.

In order to focus your Taurus energy positively, use the following list as a guide.

1. Try not to focus too intensely on owning things.
2. When you are getting too stuck in your ways, try to make one small change, just to prove you can!
3. Allow partners some space, even if it's only one night a week apart.
4. Do something out of your comfort zone now and then.

5. A couple of times a year, write a list of your positive points and why others love you to remind yourself you are valuable.

GEMINI: THE COMMUNICATOR

Your Spiritual Lesson: You have something to say, so make your words count.

This mutable air sign is the most light and flexible of all the astrological signs. You came into this life carrying the traits of the communicator with you, a memory of your sun sign being Gemini in the last life. Known as the messenger, your job would have been to pass on information, and you still give the appearance of someone on the move, someone light and airy, talkative and fun, cheerful and friendly, who is hard to pin down to a time, a place, or any form of commitment.

This is because in the last life, you inhabited this zodiac sign so well that you now naturally exhibit Gemini traits and filter everything you think and do through its familiar and comfortable characteristics. Regardless of your sun sign in this life, Gemini is your comfort. Even if you are a serious and committed Scorpio or an emotional and caring Cancer sun, people will only perceive your casual, playful, and light-hearted view of the world at first.

Geminis are renowned for saying one thing and doing another. Indeed, you did mean to be there for a meeting, or to phone a friend when you promised to, or to meet for coffee at a certain time, but you either forgot or got caught up in something else. The fact is, your life is an amazing balancing act of juggling a huge amount. Mostly, you are juggling ideas. You are an ideas and words person, a visionary, so you excel at bringing a fresh perspective to old concepts. But once an idea has been shared with the right people, you leave someone else to handle the details. Your attention span is short, and you like to flit off like a butterfly to the next exciting or interesting thing you've noticed. With so many interests and hobbies, you only have time to skim the surface before growing bored and moving on. Focus is only held when you are quickly sifting through pertinent facts; deep investigation is of no interest to you.

The thing is, as a communicator and messenger, your astrological job is to keep on the move, mentally and physically. Prior to our modern technological world, information had to be physically carried by horse or foot, and word of mouth was incredibly important. Go back farther, to ancient times, and oral knowledge was the only method of communication, with generation after generation telling stories and singing songs about their history. It was the sign of Gemini who had the important job of remembering and passing on these messages, so it is vital to understand that although people get frustrated with your inability to stick to a place and time, you have another task altogether—astrologically, you are not meant to be staying around.

People who don't understand this may become annoyed by your inability to stick to a plan or to see something through from beginning to end. But you won't be around to hear their annoyed words—you'll be long gone. Anything that gets heavy scares you. That's because your intellectual mind has an amazing ability to separate logic from emotion. Ruled by Mercury, you deal with a problem and discard the connected feeling. You can't understand why other people cannot do the same. The way you perceive it, others get too bogged down in a morass of sticky emotion.

Similarly, it is usually someone's mind that attracts you to them. If you stay up into the small hours talking to this person, if you relate on an intellectual level, you will want it to continue, and you *might* make a commitment, but it will be of a very loose sort. If you are able to commit easily, it's probable that you have earth sign placements to anchor you.

When you start to fall in love, you run away. You do so in the hopes that, with time, these feelings will dissipate. You much prefer to use your intellect to understand things, and love is inexplicable. Even those who love being in love cannot explain how it works, why it happens, or even what it is. You, more than any of the other signs, will try to justify love intellectually. You'll analyse, ponder, and sift—anything except feel. You consciously block emotions because they muddy the waters.

You are afraid of promising anything or making any sort of commitment. What if you change your mind? What if you wake up tomorrow and decide you'd rather do something different? You simply prefer to keep your schedule free so you can flit wherever you want. The commitment of time and energy that relationships demand feels claustrophobic, but once you do settle down, you somehow manage to make these commitments light and airy. In your ideal partnership, you will have so much freedom that it will be hard for others to determine whether or not you're single. Most Gemini risings are in relationships, but they prefer them without legal documents or written pledges. This is regardless of what your sun sign is in this life. Even a passionate, driven Scorpio sun changes after being filtered through an airy rising sign; its deep, dark passions are like a rough sea that has become smooth, with frothy bubbles and light interplay between the waves.

You have a witty way with words and try to lighten situations that get too serious. Many rising sign Geminis are in the media, because that is the modern form of communication. How can you be a messenger unless you know the very latest news? You naturally gravitate to positions in which your clever, amusing way with words is appreciated. Think television, radio, theatre, podcasts, or social media. These areas abound with Geminis who keep abreast of each and every change, every nuance of cultural movement. Keenly receptive and intelligent, you have no trouble picking out the pertinent points, of knowing which fad or phase or fashion will be the next big thing. You are adept at presenting, speaking, and making people laugh. You could act or sing professionally—you are incredibly versatile—but you prefer light-hearted conversation.

Your symbol is the twins. People think you are unreliable and changeable because of this symbol, but that's not the reason—you're changeable because you are the messenger of the zodiac. With that being said, you do have two sides to you. One sees in black, the other white. Geminis often make comments that are opposites. One day you may pick a side, only to reverse your stance the next day. People often wonder what you *do* believe because you express opposing opinions easily. That's because you always see both sides and have no particular interest in believing either. In the moment, you may believe something, but by tomorrow you won't. Therefore, it is easy for people to think you are a liar. In fact, you are not deliberately lying—you *did* believe that thing when you said it.

The twins are also responsible for your mood swings. Yes, even you are prone to moods. Usually, it's because your butterfly wings are being clipped by someone. Your tongue can be brutal if you feel thwarted or annoyed with someone. This is the "bad" twin. It appears now and then, using cutting words and sarcasm to make a point. You are a wordsmith of the top order and can use this tendency to your advantage if you choose a suitable profession, like professional critic or comedian.

Each rising sign has a spiritual purpose. Your messenger quality and your clever sifting of ideas is truly important in our world, but it is also easy for you to lose yourself in a make-believe world. This is the danger area with Gemini. If you have a Gemini sun and a Gemini rising sign, it could be because you got lost in the last life. Those with the sun in the first house are being given another chance to get it right. This time, there will be no hiding place; you are who you are and must express your Gemini qualities.

So, by all means, tell jokes and keep things light, but seek ways to make your words count so they're not just meaningless chatter. Be a writer, a teacher, or a communicator in some capacity. Your true calling is to be a teacher, because Gemini rules the third house of education and learning. It is incredible how many Geminis are teachers. If you choose to be a media person, make sure you are passing on important information and not just gossiping. Ensure that your words carry a real message. Then you will be fulfilling the true purpose of your rising sign.

In order to focus your Gemini energy positively, use the following list as a guide.

1. When you make an appointment, write it down, and check your schedule every morning.

2. Choose a career that is important, like teaching or speaking, to make sure your words count.

3. Now and then, see something through to the end, just to prove you can.

4. Avoid gossip. It may be amusing, but it can also be hurtful.

5. Remember the phrase "What you give out, you get back." Think about what you say and why you are saying it.

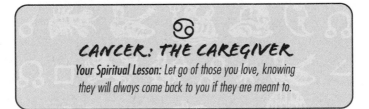

CANCER: THE CAREGIVER

Your Spiritual Lesson: *Let go of those you love, knowing they will always come back to you if they are meant to.*

The sign of Cancer rules the fourth house of the home and family, and it is ruled by the moon, making this is a very emotive sign. The moon is a receptive, intuitive, sensitive, caring, and watery planet, awash with feelings. This is why

Cancerians are credited with being so tender-hearted and easily upset by the words and actions of others. If you have a Cancer rising sign, the sign of Cancer is your safety net in this life. You can fall back on Cancer characteristics while you learn all the lessons of your new chart.

Cancer is a sign that desires to provide nourishment and warmth to all, to draw everyone they meet into their "family" and make them feel valued and special. This is the sign that nurtures the world. Each astrological sign has a purpose, and your sign is the caregiver. You gather those who are struggling in life and take them under your wing, like a mother hen, showing them that not everyone is selfish and mean, that some people are truly caring, genuine, and kind. Your feelings come straight from your heart, and it hurts you to see anyone suffering. You are the first one to go to someone's aid. That's why so many Cancers are doctors, nurses, paramedics, or counsellors—Cancers work in the caring professions in whatever way they can. Your whole purpose in life, the thing that brings you personal joy, is alleviating suffering.

This compassionate stance is as natural to you as breathing, but some of the other signs feel smothered or trapped by your watery approach. And when people try to distance themselves from your care—which they see as overprotective—you are prone to think of it as a personal attack. Anyone who thinks you are too emotional is quickly dismissed as unfeeling, but it is all a matter of perspective. Some signs just aren't equipped for the emotional content you require. (Fire signs believe all problems are solved by taking action, earth signs by waiting for a while, and air signs like to intellectualize their emotions. But the other two water signs, Scorpio and Pisces, will be right there with you!) This is why Cancerians appear so touchy. Because you are open to so many emotional nuances, you often see a problem where there isn't one, and you react with hurt feelings. You take things personally. This rising sign often confuses the two words most associated with it: feeling and emotion. Feelings are necessary and make you receptive and understanding, but the emotions that come with it can overwhelm you, and others, at times.

You, more than any other sign, seek to find yourself in others. You judge yourself by how many people you've helped and by how many close friends you have, friends who really understand you. When your soothing, warm, and receptive personality is reciprocated and appreciated by another, it makes you feel secure and valued.

People with a Cancer rising sign are often conduits for others. Complete strangers will be moved to confide in you, telling you all sorts of things they may have never told anyone else—such is your receptivity. People instinctively know you'd never tell anyone what they said, break a confidence, or use what they said against them, and they're right. You know how painful betrayal is. This makes you a completely trustworthy friend and partner who is equally genuine when counselling a stranger (and this will happen frequently).

You like being such a kind person, one who understands everyone's problems, who, in fact, enjoys nothing more than emotional discussions and finding kindred spirits. This is your comfort zone. No matter what your sun sign is in this lifetime, you use your Cancer rising as a shield to fend off intruders until you are sure you can trust them. Because Cancer is ruled by the moon, you are very intuitive about people and their motives. Even if your sun sign is a detached, cerebral air sign in this life, you won't allow anyone who does not have genuine feelings to get close to you. Your sensitivity is such that you'd rather be alone than have unfeeling people in your life.

Your symbol is the crab, that creature that scuttles sideways rather than going straight to the point. You hide your tenderness behind a tough outer shell, hoping people won't see how vulnerable you are. In fact, your sign is cardinal, which means you are proactive and perfectly capable of making changes in your life if the need arises. You are tougher than you look, and you have to be. Anyone as sensitive and soft as you needs some inner strength to cope, otherwise you'd collapse as people unknowingly trample all over you, dismissing your feelings as over-the-top and saying things that hurt (probably without meaning to, because our world is a tough place).

Others can shake off an argument. You can't. You'll brood and grieve and wonder why they were so unkind when you've only ever been nice to them. If you didn't need people so much, your inclination would be to stop talking to people, but you simply must be of assistance. Each time you get hurt, you'll cry and dwell on how cruel people are, but it won't be long before you climb back into your shell and return to the world around you, because when you're not helping people, it feels like your whole purpose in life is missing.

You endeavour to nurture every single person, but you can wear yourself out in this eternal effort because there is no end to the neediness of others. Plus, whereas they will recover and move on, you'll go looking for the next person to help because you simply cannot help it. This is exhausting. As you learn your new sun sign traits, you will probably cut back on these efforts. You will recognize that even a bottomless pit of love would not be enough for the millions of lost souls you want to understand and save. Even with the best will in the world, you cannot help everyone, and the older you get, the more you will concentrate your efforts. You will learn that you cannot give yourself to everyone all the time, and you will reserve your love for those who truly benefit from your loving support.

There is another important learning curve with this rising sign, and it is especially true if you have your sun in Cancer. Your lesson in this life is to learn that you cannot hold on to people. Helping others is your specialty, but you need to recognize when the time has come to let them go. Let people find their own footing in the world. It is hard to lose someone important, but you will come to appreciate that we are all on our own path, and as much as you don't want to admit it to yourself, you know it will probably deviate from yours at some point. Hence, the challenge for you is to learn to let go of those you love as they seek new experiences. We are often told that if you cling to someone, they strive to break free, but if you open the door for them, they will return of their own accord. This is a huge—but certainly hard—lesson that the sign of Cancer has for you. Give them your all, then let them go. Eventually, all your love will come back a thousandfold.

In order to focus your Cancer energy positively, use the following list as a guide.

1. Be aware you cannot help everyone. Focus on those who actively seek your assistance.
2. Choose a career that allows you to express your caring nature.

3. Remember that others have their own path, and it may not always be the same as yours.

4. Tell people, nicely, when they have hurt you— don't bottle it up.

5. Learn to let people go.

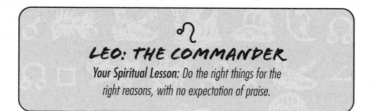

LEO: THE COMMANDER

Your Spiritual Lesson: Do the right things for the right reasons, with no expectation of praise.

Leo is a very powerful sign because it is ruled by the sun itself. You have within you a fund of joy and happiness, and you need to express it on the large stage of life. It is almost impossible to suppress the sun, and it is a sorry sight to see a Leo who is not able to share the warmth, loyalty, and affection that springs from within for whatever reason.

Leos are like a light that switches on when other people are around; this sign commands a compelling force. Any contact with Leo, the sun, or the area of life Leo rules (the fifth house) boosts personality, inner joy, and a need to express oneself. It is hard, then, for Leo risings to contain the bubbling *joie de vivre* within. It is best expressed on the stage (which is why so many Leos are actors) or in the many fields connected to it, though any form of self-expression is healthy for you. The arts are a good example because you are creating something from within, be it a painting, a sculpture, or a book. Children also fall under the umbrella of this sign and house because of their unalloyed and uncomplicated joy, and in fact, they are an act of creation. Unsurprisingly, Leos often choose to work with children and enjoy bringing out the fun, creative side of young people.

The house ruled by Leo, the fifth house, is in what is called the *collective* area at the bottom of the birth chart, which means you need to express your personality within your local environment. Hence, you should work with people. You enjoy partaking in activities in your local area, doing all you can to be an active, participating member in your community in whatever role will enable you to express the full force of your personality. If a community centre hosts a fundraiser, a church needs someone to organize an event, or a local group seeks a spokesperson, you are the person most likely to step forward.

But Leos are leaders in any field. You can't help gravitating towards a leadership role wherever you choose to work. You enjoy being a spokesperson because being in charge comes naturally. Leadership often requires delegating, and you enjoy this task. In truth, not many Leos like getting their hands dirty with menial tasks, and you have a way with people that manages to charmingly cajole them into doing the stuff you'd rather not.

Leo is the sign of royalty, and it's easy to see why. Wherever you go, you carry an aura of capability and assurance. People stand back and allow you to take centre stage. They defer to you because of your self-confidence, and you are not shy about assuming the role of leader. And, the truth is, a lot of people don't want to be in charge of things; they prefer leaving that task to someone else, and you were made for this role. Hence, there are lots of vacant positions just waiting for you.

At its very best, Leo is full of charisma, magnetism, charm, and style. Because this is your rising sign, your sun sign in the last life, you naturally express your confident, can-do nature because it feels comfortable. If you have the sun in Leo as well, it is because you failed to learn the lessons of Leo properly the first time. You are being given another chance to get it right.

So, where did you go wrong? Well, along with your innate ability to shine and stand out from the crowd comes an assumption that you will use your talents correctly. It is very easy for a Leo to become overly confident, ego-driven, and attracted to glamour, glitter, and drama. It is tempting to allow power to go to your head, and this is the pitfall you must avoid. You believe that you can save everyone, and your need for recognition for every little thing you do for others results in the expectation of continual thanks—preferably praise—which becomes a necessity. This becomes a toxic cycle of working yourself into the ground in an effort to receive a bit of admiration.

All astrological signs have downsides and danger areas, and this is Leo's: a weakness to flattery and the innate need for people to be outwardly thankful for what you do. This makes for uncomfortable relationships because you do more and more, then get aggrieved when your partner does not notice all your hard work. In fact, they probably have noticed, but that isn't enough for you. You need to hear it said aloud, and unless they know you expect this, you may end up feeling very sorry for yourself. Remember that your loved ones may be blithely unaware that you need outward praise. Given the praise you feel you so richly deserve, you glow; denied it, you slump. If you feel really unappreciated, you will move on to someone who does seem to value you. You do not do this out of unkindness. You leave because it is making you ill not to have your talents recognized and appreciated; being ignored or taken for granted damages your sense of well-being.

So, how can you gain the recognition you need while accepting it isn't always possible for people to praise you? Emulate strong leaders. The very best of them earn respect and admiration for their brave and noble deeds and, because they stand inside their own personalities, they do not base their sense of self-worth on what other people think. They do what they feel is right and proper based on what emanates from within. You are capable of the very best of human nature (rescuing people in trouble, organizing charitable events, inspiring people), but only if you use your incredible talents properly. If you focus solely on wealth, applause, constant thanks, and praise—all of which are so necessary for your well-being—it can make you conceited.

Your inner nature is to master life, to rise to challenges, to boldly go forth. Your task is to properly use your sincerity, loyalty, and decency for the benefit of mankind, not for the aggrandizement of yourself. And you should do this because of an inner sense of moral rightness, not with the purpose of gaining appreciation. These higher aims naturally bring appreciation and reward anyway, so the better and higher you aim, the more you gain that respect you so need. It isn't actually praise you need—it is respect. Respect comes when your actions are worthy of it. So, that should be your aim.

If your sun sign is not Leo, you achieved this goal in the last life. You protected those you loved and cared for and sheltered them from all harm, and their respect and regard fuelled you to even greater efforts. If your sun and rising are in Leo, this is an ongoing pursuit. Like your symbol, the lion, make sure you keep others safe by using your talents in the way they were intended to be used. Lean on your loyalty and sense of moral duty and rightness. Do the right thing because you can, not because you want praise.

Surround yourself with people who see the best in you. The best of Leo is, without question, the absolute best there is. Most Leos have an adoring family who know how much you do for them and highly value your sacrifices. There is nothing wrong with enjoying an expensive meal or driving around in a flashy car, but do not lose sight of the things that truly matter in life. Remain focused on the important things and be a beacon of light and warmth in the world.

In order to focus your Leo energy positively, use the following list as a guide.

1. Choose a career that fully utilizes your talents, one where respect can be earned.
2. Do things because you can, not because of the end result.
3. When someone doesn't say thank you, try to let it go.
4. Avoid overreacting by staying grounded.
5. Don't be led away by false glamour. Never lose sight of your true path.

ᛗ
VIRGO: THE DISCERNING CRITIC
Your Spiritual Lesson: Be discerning for a reason, for a higher cause.

Virgo is a mutable earth sign and is renowned for being fussy. Anyone who knows anything about astrology knows that the Virgos of this world are organized, critical, and judgmental; this is the astrological sign of the perfectionist. If you have a Virgo rising sign, everything you say and do (and everything others say and do) is certainly filtered through this fastidious lens.

Although Virgo is an earth sign, it has many airy qualities. The earth element shows you are grounded in reality: you seek to bring order to your own world and to the world around you. Hence, you put your shoulder to the wheel and do your very best to sort out the messes that abound. This is an earthy challenge because you see the practical details and work with them, but you use your mind to do so.

Virgos are thinkers. Analysing comes naturally to you. You notice everything; you think about everything. Nothing passes you by without reflection and consideration. This makes you selective. Why? Because you see disorder everywhere. But one lone soul cannot bring order to everyone and everything, so you must choose your mental battles. Otherwise, you can become completely overwhelmed by the tasks you set for yourself.

Our world is chaotic in every sense. We hurtle through space on a ball of debris. The human race has tried to organize itself into a cohesive society in order to feed itself, procreate, and continue being the dominant species on the planet, but the truth is we are hanging on to this organization by a thread; everywhere, humanity threatens to crumble into anarchy and chaos. And no one sees this more clearly than you.

This is where you excel. Modest, unassuming, and with no desire for the spotlight or any sort of recognition, you do your best to make sure these structures stand firm by checking and rechecking the details. Whatever the task, you take pride and joy in making sure everything works well. Okay, maybe you don't actually care about the bigger picture (this will depend on the rest of your chart), but you will certainly focus closer to home. Your first self-imposed task is to make sure your own world is neat and tidy. You start with yourself. As a Virgo, you are probably health conscious. After all, being slovenly is, in your eyes, disorganized. It means letting go. You need control, but to have control in any other area, you need to start with yourself. So, you control your health to the best of your ability, striving to meet certain goals you've set for yourself. People might think you are judgmental, but you are a far harsher judge of yourself. You watch yourself all the time. Only when you have yourself under control do you allow your laser vision to scan outward, and then it is those around you who come under scrutiny: your friends and family.

Not many people think of Virgo as a controlling sign, but it is. You are far more subtle at it than a Scorpio or Taurus, but you still take charge of your environment, both at home and at work, to make sure it's neat and tidy and running efficiently. Anyone with a Virgo partner will smile at this; they know who is in charge! Virgos are benign dictators. Nevertheless, your partners will have their faults pointed out and will be left in no doubt that they need to straighten up their act. You cannot live with someone who throws their clothes onto a heap on the floor or leaves half-empty cups of coffee scattered about, or even someone who occasionally spills something on the pristine carpet. That mark will be pointed out for sure.

You are selective of your partners in an attempt to keep this from happening in the first place. You couldn't bear to have a partner who was slovenly in any way; it would drive you mad. You like those in your life to be as clean, neat, and tidy as you, and preferably as focused on their health. You rarely allow someone into your world who has not been thoroughly vetted. All of us are careful about who we allow into our inner circle to some degree, but you are a harsher critic than most. And once you allow someone to know you better, they will be kept on their toes and held to an unrelenting high standard.

The thing is, although you are an intrinsically kind person, you simply cannot refrain from noticing things, and once you've seen them, you find it impossible not to remark on them. Your sign is ruled by Mercury, which is the verbal planet, the planet of communication. And, if this planet in your chart is in an astrological sign that is outspoken, your words can sound very critical. For example, Sagittarians are renowned for being blunt, and Aries always speak their minds, so these are just two positions of Mercury that may exacerbate your already-critical tendencies. You may have a waspish tongue and a very clever but brutal way with words, which can reduce others to a jelly. No one enjoys being criticized, but you simply cannot help it. You are driven to keep things neat and simply *must* speak out. In most cases, you try to be gentle and kind in your remarks.

Your cleverness with words can be used to great effect as a comedian, writer, actor, or public speaker—but you will have your words edited and honed and keep your delivery cool and polished. When you present yourself to the world, you always make sure to put your best foot forward. Although you ask others to meet your high and exacting standards, you cannot take criticism yourself. You are your own harshest critic anyway, so to have things pointed out by someone else undermines you completely. Yours is not an ego-driven sign, and you are very vulnerable to personal attack yourself. You are actually quite fragile.

The difficulty with this rising sign is that you take disorder personally. In an effort to isolate yourself from anything and anyone that is too crude, harsh, or unruly, you tend to compartmentalize everything, thus fragmenting your personality. You cannot then fully integrate with partners and friends; there is always an eye looking for fault. This can scupper the very best of friendships.

Your real task—and if your sun is not in Virgo in this life, you achieved this—is to judge only yourself, leaving others to sort themselves out. By all means, form your ideas and opinions and claim the moral high ground; live the best you can and meet your own high expectations for yourself. Do this instead of forcing your perfectionism on others. If you don't, you will exhaust yourself, upset others with your criticisms, and be perceived as fussy. When you use your perfectionist tendencies for good, you can clearly see where change is necessary and make a proper difference in the world. Instead of pointing out flaws, you suddenly have a higher purpose to pursue.

When your rising sign energy is being channelled properly, your need for control is lessened. All you really need to control is yourself, and this you do most efficiently. You are the highest pinnacle of what a human can be, and you shortchange yourself by becoming involved in things that do not concern you. You are conscientious, hardworking, dutiful, and modest. You have so many wonderful innate qualities, and because you are so organized and efficient, you are a magnet to people. Yet, you do lack self-confidence, especially in romantic matters.

Virgo is a contradiction in love. On the one hand, you'd like a partner who gets your need for cleanliness and order, so you are, of course, very selective, but yours is one of the earthiest signs. Therefore, sex is very important to you. This is a contradiction because sex is not tidy, and it means letting go, which seems to go against everything you believe in. Perhaps it is more of a release for you than any other sign. Because you restrain yourself so much in day-to-day life, you need to simply let go and allow yourself to be human now and then, just like the rest of us.

If your sun and rising signs are in Virgo, you are again being asked to focus inward. Any planet in the first house is on show, so you cannot hide behind your Virgo rising sign this time—you are forced to display yourself. This time, aim high. Aim for purity, streamline your own world, find a career or place where your incredibly discerning nature will make a real difference, create your own highest ideals, and concentrate on yourself.

People with the same sun and rising sign are often famous. If this is the case, use your talents for the betterment of mankind.

In order to focus your Virgo energy positively, use the following list as a guide.

1. Try not to get drawn into the small stuff.
2. Now and then, have a go at ignoring something that isn't right, like a wonky picture.
3. Although others may annoy you, avoid criticising them; think how you'd feel if someone said the same thing to you.
4. Concentrate on being the best possible version of yourself.
5. Choose a career where your discerning nature can be used for the benefit of all.

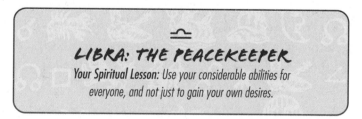

LIBRA: THE PEACEKEEPER

Your Spiritual Lesson: Use your considerable abilities for everyone, and not just to gain your own desires.

Libra is ruled by Venus, so your overriding desire is peace and harmony. As the world is usually anything but, you extend a lot of energy trying to create this in your home, your working life, and your relationships. Venus-ruled people are usually blessed with personal beauty and the need to lead a gentle, balanced existence free from strife and aggression. To obtain this delicate balance is an art in itself, which is why your symbol is the scales. Sometimes referred to as the scales of justice, this symbol is still used in courts of law. The scales describe your desire to make objective, reasoned, and balanced judgements. To do this requires a certain amount of detachment and logic, which is why Libra is an air sign. Air signs are thinkers, so you spend a lot of your time coming up with solutions that will (hopefully) keep everyone happy.

Your energy is spent on pleasing people so that others are happy because when they are happy, you are happy. The problem with giving so much to others in order to have harmony means you run the risk of losing who you really are. If you continue trying to be all things to all people, one day you may wake up and wonder who *you* are. Are you just a reflection of everyone else? Libra is probably one of the least selfish of the astrological signs because of this need for peace. Compromise is inherent in your nature. You will do almost anything to keep the peace, and if giving in to others is the price to pay, you pay it willingly. In effect, then, you appear entirely unselfish. But you aren't. Not really.

Why? Well, Libra is the sign of lawyers. Lawyers are clever. They use words in a way that can make the guilty seem innocent and the innocent appear guilty. It is all a matter of how its phrased and presented, and this is your forte: the way you cleverly use words. Without raising your voice, or appearing to argue, you get your way with beguiling charm; this is your weapon, and you've known how to use it from the moment you were born. So, anyone who starts to feel sorry for this lovely, gentle sign need not worry. The truth is, you are adept at manipulating people to reach your own ends. But you choose your battles. The things that you can tolerate, you do, thus allowing the other person to believe they are getting their own way. When someone suggests an activity or an idea you don't like, you will appear to agree, but you will immediately start figuring out how to get the result you'd prefer without any sort of outward confrontation. The last thing you want to do is make waves in the harmonious atmosphere you've created all around you, so your mind goes into overdrive trying to devise a plan that suits everyone *and* gives you what you want. So, yes, you do compromise, but your cleverness means you rarely have to.

While you are mentally striving to bring everything into harmony, your scales can dip from side to side, but eventually they level out. And when your scales are balanced, no one is more outwardly obliging, sensible, and reasonable. You want to live in peaceful coexistence with everyone. But it is not easy, because to do this usually means being removed from the rougher elements of life, and that requires money. Your ideal haven is rarely found amongst those who struggle to make ends meet. If you meet someone who can offer you a better life, you will grab on to them—as long as you like them.

In no circumstances will you date someone if they are coarse or vulgar or noisy. The last thing you want is someone unappealing on your arm—your partner is a reflection of you! Your partner must have a certain *je ne sais quoi* because you want them to be admired. And, the truth is, your partner must have money. You are only attracted to people who have something to offer you. Your love of designer clothes, of the best hotels, of wining and dining at the "in" place in town, of hiring people to do your chores for you, means your aim is a high-end lifestyle.

In return, you offer the very best; you will never fail to make an impression with your clothes, your innate style, and your class. You behave impeccably and can go anywhere without fear of making a faux pas. Whatever circumstances you find yourself in, you can use your charm to great effect. You are selective, discerning, and tasteful.

But, despite being ruled by the planet of love, you are cool in your relationships. Having fun is great. Going to amazing hotels is wonderful, and you adore your designer house, but when it comes to the more intimate moments of the relationship, you only tolerate them. Even if your partner has provided the wherewithal to fund your preferred lifestyle, you find it hard to enjoy the nitty-gritty of the physical side of love. Libra is an air sign, and all air signs prefer thinking about sex to actually doing it. Sex will be a perfunctory act, quickly over with, unless there are earthy planets in your chart.

Love is universal, and you have the capacity to spread love wherever you go—not the love of the flesh, but the love of the mind. When you only think about how things can benefit you, you lose your perspective by making your innate gifts of compromise and love personal instead of using them for the benefit of all. This is the spiritual challenge of Libra rising. The love within should flow out to everyone instead of being used selfishly, for you alone to gain your desired ends.

Always, you have your eye on the mirror. You really do care what other people think, and you really do believe that they envy you. But, if you stand back and see it objectively, you will realize that creating envy is a negative thing. And, in truth, people don't envy others who appear to have more: the spiritually unevolved dislike you for it, and the spiritually evolved pity you for being so attached to the unimportant. It rarely engenders the response you so desire.

It is easier for you than other signs to get drawn into the allure of the impersonal world, to see yourself as only a reflection of others. If you feel your attractiveness waning, you may have affairs just to remind yourself you are desirable. Looking beautiful, wearing designer fashion, and owning what everyone else is buying are externals that forever lure you away from your spiritual path. If your sun is in Libra in this life, your real lessons have yet to be grasped. When you have the same sun and rising sign, your true self is seen by the world—it has nowhere to hide. In this life, you are once again being asked to be the highest and best you can be.

If you let all your love flow though you, you are in tune with the very best of human nature. If you foreswear the need for designer labels and showing off assets, beauty, and possessions, you can pursue a higher purpose. By all means, create a haven for yourself, but then use your harmonious skills for a good cause: negotiate peace for warring nations, bring together people who are estranged, utilize your verbal talents to get people off the streets, or become a politician and advocate changes that bring peace and harmony to your fellow man. There is no end to what someone with such an astute, clever mind and boundless love can do. Don't keep this all for yourself. Spread it around!

In order to focus your Libra energy positively, use the following list as a guide.

1. Find a career that uses your talents at their highest vibration.

2. Try to avoid the pull of the impersonal world.

3. Don't forget that everyone has value, not just those with money.

4. Resist the urge to get people to do the things you'd rather not.

5. Don't let others walk all over you. Stand your ground when it's important to do so.

♏
SCORPIO: THE RESEARCHER
Your Spiritual Lesson: *Always seek the higher path.*

This is one of the most enigmatic rising signs, and therefore it is not easy to explain in simple terms, because nothing about this astrological sign is straightforward. Certainly, those with this rising sign (and, therefore, their sun in Scorpio in the last life) have greater depths of knowledge and purpose than any other sign in the zodiac.

Let's start with the obvious. Scorpio does not like to reveal itself to anyone, so even when it is your rising sign, you prefer to hide your intentions and motives. This is odd, because you are already using your rising sign as a form of disguise and protection, yet you want to be even more secretive by not letting people see that you have Scorpio rising. And this is usually the only way others can spot if you have this rising sign, because you give nothing away!

That is not to say you aren't friendly and kind. You may be. But no one will ever know if this is the real you or just an act. Even those who have known you a long time—and those who *think* they know you—don't. You always keep your motives hidden, even from those you have spent a lifetime with. That may be because you don't like your motivations much. Let's use an example: Maybe you are someone who wants the best in life in terms of money and lifestyle, but you feel that you are revealing too much by explaining this to people, or by letting them see how much it would mean to you. There could be a number of reasons you don't want them to know this. Scorpio risings who are highly evolved may feel this is a base desire in the grand scheme of things, and despite needing security, feel it is not a high enough purpose to put on display. Or maybe you have fears that you won't achieve your aims and then you'd feel stupid, and you simply can't bear to be exposed like that—as someone who has failed. Or, for less-evolved Scorpios, you may be using others for your own ends. By revealing your plans, you will scupper them.

Whatever level you are operating at (and you probably shift and change between all of them at different times), letting others know your thoughts, see your aims, or suss your motives is too exposing. You'd rather try and then fail in private so that you don't lose face. The fact is, you are a loner. You make a decision, and then you alone pay the price. The buck stops with you. You don't share your dreams; you keep them close. That way, the outcome is yours alone to mourn or celebrate.

The reason this self-protection matters so much is because Scorpio is a fixed water sign. When water is held in a restricted area, in one place, it becomes deep and dark. And this is how you feel everything in life: with such depths of emotion and passion it is overwhelming. It is this ultra-sensitivity that makes you so self-protective. You loathe feeling shame or embarrassment in public, so you shrink from situations in which this might happen. On the surface you keep a calm demeanour; you baulk at outwardly displaying your feelings. You can be sick with nerves or pumped up with pride, but you will show neither.

Someone finding out something you want kept private and then putting it in writing, or telling someone about it, would horrify you. That would mean you've lost control of the situation. It would be out of your hands, and knowing there would be nothing you could do about that is very scary. When you decide what you tell people, you can control it, but once it is out there, it's impossible to put the genie back in the bottle. It is this that terrifies you.

The rising sign is a mask, and most people use this mask as a display. They are happy to show the characteristics of the astrological sign they are so comfortable with when first meeting someone. Not you. The opposite is true. Instead of revealing yourself, you stare out from inside the mask and analyse everyone and everything that comes to you from the outside world. You have an incredibly powerful intuition, verging on psychic. You instinctively know all sorts of intuitive things. With your scanning radar, little bits of knowledge come to you, and you interpret them quickly and correctly. You may not actually see everything, but you *feel* it; your intuitive knowledge is that highly attuned. Plus, you quickly identify people who only want something from you.

Scorpio risings are rarely duped, but it does happen, and from then on you will be even more wary. The person who betrayed you or let you down will never escape retribution because there is no revenge more complete than yours. You bide your time, then strike. Absolutely no one who betrays you gets away with it. Sometimes your revenge will be so subtle that it comes years later and apparently via another source. The highly evolved Scorpio does not engage in revenge, instead letting things play out on their own, but you'll still feel an inner satisfaction when your "enemy" gets their comeuppance.

If you trust that a new person in your life will not use anything they find out about you in a negative way, you may be a bit friendlier. You may even accept them as a friend. Generally, Scorpio risings don't have a lot of friends—only those who have passed this test. Even so, your friends will never really know you. It's likely you will show different parts of yourself to different people, but one person, even a beloved long-term partner, will still not be privy to every secret in your heart.

You live life at a high emotional intensity, investing everything you have in every little thing you do. No matter if its learning about fungi, delving into the mysteries of space, or assessing a new person, you leave no stone unturned. You simply have to give it your all. And you love a challenge. The harder the task, the stronger your determination to overcome it.

Scorpio is the most powerful rising sign to have. The aim—and you have already achieved this if you do not have your sun in Scorpio is this life—is self-mastery. Your inner strength is formidable, you can overcome anything you wish to through sheer willpower and resolve. But your desires are also great, as is your need to control. It would be so easy to use what you intuitively sense from others; you have the capacity to see many levels of existence. Out of all the astrological signs, you have the deepest dark side and the purest light side, and you are aware of this. You can sense both, and you must choose, at every step of the way in life, whether to give in to base desires of jealousy, revenge, manipulation, and control, or to do what you are meant to: choose the higher path. All the time you are testing your own powers of inner strength in order to overcome any weakness; every challenge life throws at you is seen a test of your willpower and resolve.

By resisting the desire to act in a negative or destructive way, you can rise spiritually higher than anyone else (except perhaps Pisces, for whom forgiveness comes so naturally). If you have your sun and rising sign in Scorpio, there are still lessons to learn. Self-control and mastery are your lessons. Use your powerful inner drives to control your dark side by always choosing the higher path. Lift yourself towards the light by strictly using your knowledge and strength with purity of intention.

In order to focus your Scorpio energy positively, use the following list as a guide.

1. Walk away when people hurt you.
2. Choose never to seek revenge.
3. Forgive, forgive, forgive!
4. Resist the urge to use your powers for anything other than self-mastery.
5. Choose a career where you can work alone yet achieve greatness.

♐ SAGITTARIUS: THE TRUTH-SEEKER

Your Spiritual Lesson: The truth is within you.

This mutable fire sign imbues you with scattered energy. Think of a fire on a hillside blown in many directions by a blustery wind—this pretty much describes the energies you have within you. Although your energy is scattered from time to time, you are not a lazy person by any stretch of the imagination. This is the one sign that likes their day booked from dawn 'til dusk. There is something about an empty day that scares you, so you keep your schedule jammed full of activities, people to meet, and places to go.

You are so active, people often wonder what you are running away from, but in fact, you are not running *from* something, but *to* something—anything. That's because you have an insatiable thirst for knowledge, and your way of finding it is by exploring every single avenue of opportunity. That person might know something you didn't; that activity might reveal something about yourself or life; that meeting might prove enlightening. Every single thing in life is full of the potential for knowledge, and you hate to miss a chance.

The reason you feel this way is because Sagittarius is the ruler of the ninth house, and this is the house of higher learning. In enlightened terms, it is the search for truth. People with an emphasis on this house in their chart become solitary researchers and higher-institution lecturers. They become journalists who travel to distant corners of the world to discover mysteries still unexplored—all those polar explorers of the past, all those who hacked their way into the jungles of the world in search of hidden cultures and new knowledge of flora and fauna, these were ninth-house, Sagittarian-like people. Whatever field you choose to pursue, you have a natural ability and instinct to know more, to be the one who pushes the boundaries into unexplored territory. Aquarius does the same, but in an inspired, flash-of-genius way, whereas you keep searching for the root of truth and enlightenment.

This is the energy you are imbued with: a constant, unceasing search for knowledge. All Sagittarians are explorers, even if your boundaries of exploration don't extend beyond your local area. Exploration isn't always a conscious thing; it is the drive to keep on the move, and it motivates you to always say yes to things no matter how tired you are.

Truth is a rarity in our world. People prevaricate and lie all the time, usually to keep the peace or to protect themselves. From white lies to lying to a partner about an affair or deceiving people via scams, our world is a place where the real, unvarnished truth hardly exists. Yet, truth is important to you. Your sign alone speaks it. You alone want to say, "No, that dress doesn't suit you," and often, you do! It may hurt someone, but honesty is more important to you than anything else.

This motivation is the reason you search for the real truths of mankind. Naturally, you started with yourself: a beacon of truth in a shady world of lies and misconceptions, deliberate or otherwise. You threw back the veil and remained truthful, even in delicate situations. But what is the truth? This is the question that stirs within you.

Subconsciously, you sense something bigger out there, something more, something larger than anyone can understand, and you want to know what it is. How can you ever hope to find out when so many people have their own truths and beliefs? In order to make any sense of it, you listen to everyone's opinion, and in each, you find a nugget of truth. By doing so much, interacting with so many, and exploring far and wide, you believe that one day, the meaning of everything will become clear (you certainly hope!).

In the meantime, you may be attracted to various sects or religious movements or groups who believe in a different way of existing in an effort to find the real truth. Thus, you scatter yourself too thin. You are so busy looking that you may actually miss what you are looking for. You listen but do not hear because you are thinking about the next thing on your agenda. Or, you mistake manipulation for knowledge. If someone claims to know the secret and reveals small parts of it to you, you become hooked. You can and do go down false paths because of your inability to distinguish a conman from a truly spiritual person. This is not a fault. Indeed, it is because you are so trusting that you find yourself mistakenly believing in someone or something false, but eventually you will realize that even the most basic truth is difficult to find, let alone the mysterious truths of our existence.

All fire signs are trusting, innocent, and without guile. Fire signs are those most easily lured by people who wish to deceive in even the smallest way. You believe what people tell you, then are completely devastated when the truth is revealed, when someone knows no more than you, despite all their flowery words. Mostly, you are devastated because they lied, because they didn't tell the truth. This is what really hurts, and it shocks you to the core.

Your symbol is the archer. He sends out arrows one after the other and wherever they land, you go. Your stable relationships suffer. How can someone so busy, with so many arrows shooting out all over the place, stay with one person, in one house, in one area, for a lifetime? Taurus might, but Sagittarius cannot. A committed relationship will take an understanding partner. They may struggle to wrap their head around the speed with which you navigate life.

You will, however, make a great parent, because your children will have full, busy, active lives—you may well wear *them* out! Endless television is not for you; you want to be doing something, and the kids will have to come along. Your children will have every experience possible, and you will be right there with them. No way you are going to miss out on some fun!

So, those of you with Sagittarius rising are busy people. You are also friendly, fun, and very accepting of people from all walks of life. You are adventurous and always learning. If you don't have your sun in Sagittarius in this life, you learnt your spiritual lesson last time, but if you do, you have a second chance to get it right. This time around, try to realize that you already have the truth within you, and that your endless search for other people's truths only dissipates your own innate inner knowing. If you stay quiet and still now and then, you will instinctively and intuitively know if people are speaking the truth because it will resonate within. You will not be fooled by false truths, and you will see through deceitful claims.

Your ruling planet is Jupiter, which is associated with gambling and luck and abundance. People assume gambling to mean betting, but in this context, it means taking a chance. You adore taking chances because you feel sure the universe has your back. It many ways, it does.

To fulfil your potential, express yourself in your eternally youthful way, full of life and happiness, and abundance will come to you. Don't rush the process of enlightenment. Feel your way around, and always allow proclaimed truths to wash over your inner being. Then and only then will you finally understand that the real truth has been inside you the whole time. Your sign rules the ninth house of esoteric wisdom, so you really do know the answers. If only you took a breather every now and then to hear them!

In order to focus your Sagittarius energy positively, use the following list as a guide.

1. Limit the number of things you do at any one time. Don't spread yourself too thin.

2. Be a teacher or educator, because your enthusiasm never wanes and will be an inspiration to others.

3. Beware of innocently trusting people who sound like they have the answers.

4. Listen to your own inner voice; your intuition will guide you.

5. Travel and explore as much as you can, but know that the answers are within.

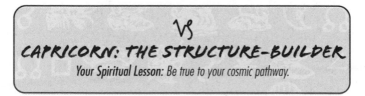

♑
CAPRICORN: THE STRUCTURE-BUILDER
Your Spiritual Lesson: Be true to your cosmic pathway.

This is one of the toughest rising signs to have. Capricorn is ruled by the planet Saturn, which is rather feared. Those who know anything about astrology have heard about Saturn's famed reputation for creating obstacles and difficulties. And it is true that those with this rising sign—or even those with Saturn in the first house—have a strong spiritual lesson to learn. If you managed to learn this lesson, your sun will not be in Capricorn; if both your sun and rising sign are Capricorn, you still have lessons to learn.

Capricorn is a cardinal earth sign. Earth signs all seek to build something. It is always something tangible and real, like money in the bank, property, or land. So, those with this rising sign will present as though they have their eye on success—not the overnight sort of success so prevalent in today's world, but that traditional, hard-working, long road to success. Capricorn never wastes its time on risky ventures or quick schemes to get rich. There is an innate knowledge that the tried and tested works and that rules and regulations set up by past generations are there for a purpose, so to follow them is wise. Therefore, you will seek to use your talents in the world in places that have stability and security, like financial institutions, politics, and long-standing, highly regarded companies. You prefer to follow the pathway of proven success. Alternatively, you may choose to work for yourself. If you do, you will offer a service that is based on traditional values, with honesty and integrity at its core. You will pride yourself on creating a family-feel amongst your workers.

The main lesson of this rising sign is to learn wisdom. Because you understand the sign of Capricorn so well, you came into this world fully aware that life requires hard work and that the passing fads and fancies of our ever-changing culture are not worth investing in. You won't want to invest money in fads, nor will you invest yourself. There is a certainty with this ascendant that you have a particular path to follow, and there is a sense of looking out at the modern world and its continually changing ideas and methods and shaking the head. You instinctively know all this will pass, and that only by sticking to the old ways, the old rules, and the old structures can you build something lasting.

This is exacerbated by a constant feeling of being watched. You may not be sure who watches, though some feel it is a deity of some sort. Whatever or whoever is watching, you feel they do so to make sure you tread the correct path, and that is why this rising sign is considered so significant. You feel there is no escape from being anything other than you are. Your moral code is extremely high, and any time you step outside it and commit an act you know is wrong, the fallout happens pretty quickly. From a young age, any transgression will have near-immediate results, and thus, by middle-age, most Capricorn risings have an inner compass that keeps them rigidly on the straight and narrow. You tread the path to true spirituality, but via tangible means.

Capricorn is often seen as the wise old parent, but for those who assume this role, like everything in their life, it is a gradual blossoming. When young, you may appear a bit old-fashioned to your contemporaries, but by the time you are all heading into midlife, your true worth becomes apparent. Somehow, you seem to grow more youthful with each passing year. And Capricorns often live a long life, being blessed with inner as well as outer strength.

Additionally, you teach by example. Not one to preach, you allow your actions to say all that is required. People will look at you and see a wise and sensible person who has broad shoulders and a lot of common sense, and many feel supported and comforted by your resilience and sense of inner certainty.

You bring your soul lessons with you from the previous lifetime, so despite having the same temptations as everyone else, your moral high ground is always reminding you when things are wrong. Thus, you have the strength to restrain yourself from making poor choices. And with your inner wisdom being so highly attuned, it's likely you are well aware of the limits allowed to you in life—and you are capable of sticking to them.

In effect, you are your own judge, and you are pretty tough on yourself. You feel you are here to do a job, and you want to do it well: no cutting corners; no skimping on anything. You work as hard as necessary and can easily eschew a party if work commitments require it. To be honest, you aren't a party lover. This is because you instinctively know that parties are mostly vanity: all that dressing up and conversation that's often self-aggrandizement. Then, there is the eating too much, drinking too much, noisy music, shouting to make conversation—none of it appeals. Your highly spiritual side looks out and sees it for what it really is: a waste of time and effort for no reward. Meaningless. You want your downtime to be quietly classy, like renting a room at a luxurious hotel, a beautifully cooked meal, meaningful conversation, and a swim in a pool that's just the right temperature. You seek activities that truly relax you and prepare you for a new day, and noisy partying is not one of them.

The lesson in this rising sign (which you have learnt if your sun is not in Capricorn) is that you are on your own pathway, and you must be true to it. You have strong convictions about what is right and what is wrong, and you easily see right through all the dross that surrounds life. In effect, you effortlessly sweep your hand across your own inner windscreen to clear it of unnecessary fog and mist.

You know you have a destiny, and you clearly know you cannot sidestep it, thus you bend your shoulder to the wheel and assume your burden. You do it willingly, knowingly, and with great wisdom. You don't waste time on those on lower spiritual levels, not because you judge them (you are aware there is no judgement among souls all striving) but because your own destiny is all you need to concern yourself with.

You are your own harshest critic and judge; you find it almost impossible to go against your own conscience. You work towards things of lasting value in your life. You want to leave a legacy behind, something that makes you feel your life has been worthwhile, that your self-imposed sacrifices were for a reason. All the time, you feel you are moving closer to your own spiritual self, so you climb higher and higher within, and as you climb, your path becomes steeper but more clearly defined. You want to die knowing you did your very best, that never once did you step from the narrow path, that you were true to you.

If your sun and rising sign are in Capricorn, you didn't fully absorb these lessons in the last life, so now there is nowhere to escape. The sun has to express itself, so you will strive to be the best you can and do the best you can, to help others along the way, and to leave a lasting legacy behind. You know life is not all about you, but about your contribution and your cosmic footprint.

Most people do not realize that the sign of Capricorn holds such spiritual depths. It truly is the hardest rising sign to have, yet in terms of spiritual growth, it is the most rewarding. True wisdom awaits.

In order to focus your Capricorn energy positively, use the following list as a guide.

1. Balance hard work with holidays and downtime.
2. Avoid judging those who do not think as you do.
3. Set times that you will start and finish each work-day to allow time for family/your partner.
4. Status is important to you, but avoid the pitfall of thinking it's the be-all and end-all.
5. It's good to do things for others, but you are allowed to indulge yourself too.

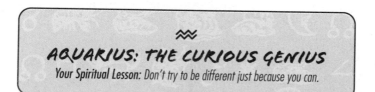

≈≈
AQUARIUS: THE CURIOUS GENIUS
Your Spiritual Lesson: *Don't try to be different just because you can.*

Enigmatic Aquarius, the one sign that is almost impossible to define. There is no such thing as a "typical Aquarius" because you consciously strive to be different. Different to everyone else, yes, but also from every other Aquarian. It is your uniqueness that is special, and as soon as you seem to be slipping into the mundane, off you go again, saying or doing something to rock the stability the rest of us need. You alone see that our world is built on shifting sands, and you enjoy nothing more than digging it out from under the rest of us and watching us slip and slide as we scrabble to hang on to our beliefs.

Aquarius is a fixed air sign. Air signs are cerebral. They think. And you think more than any other sign. But you don't think about the things everyone else does. You resonate to a different vibration altogether, whether you realize it or not. Maybe you thought everyone thinks the same way? Nope, they don't. Not at all.

For a start, you hardly give a thought to other people. This in itself is unusual because most everyone else focuses on other people: family, friends, loved ones, children, even their pets. For them, it is all about finding their place in the world amongst others: how to present well, how to gain friends, how to maintain good partnerships, how to succeed at their career, how to create a stable and happy life. This is of no interest to an Aquarius rising; it's all too prosaic. Who cares about all that? You certainly don't. You have other fish to fry.

If someone were to ask you what you're after, you wouldn't have an answer. That's because you haven't discovered what you are looking for yet, but you know it has nothing to do with human relationships and everything to do with unseen vibration and energies. This might sound like Pisces, that gentle soul who understands all things unseen, but you're not quite the same; you don't flow with the water of life like they do. You are somewhere in the realms of space, picking up on blips and forces beyond our ken. You can't describe it, nor explain it—you just feel it. The world we inhabit is far too small a space for your intellect. You wish to mentally roam, and for this reason, your physical body is rarely in the present.

This is why you have such problems with personal relationships. Human emotions are a bit beneath you. You aren't judgmental in any way whatsoever, it's just that you simply don't care what people think and do. This is not out of cruelty or meanness. It doesn't even occur to you to bring yourself down to earth to comfort the person right in front of you that is having a breakdown. You see them, you hear them (sort of), but it rarely occurs to you that they may need something from you. And, after your initial curiosity about their weird emotionalism, you decide it is too intense and walk out.

This is why anyone who expects dramatic and passionate love from an Aquarius is on a road to nowhere. Quite frankly, expecting any sort of support at all is wishful thinking. Even a traditional commitment or a normal life is off the mark. When people lean on you, they fall over. You do form relationships, but only because everyone else is doing it and you want to know what the fuss is about. The truth is, you aren't emotional nor tactile, supportive, or compassionate. Friendships are your thing, so you are more likely to marry a good friend. Even so, you never feel one hundred percent committed, yet you'll stay in a relationship if a partner does the mundane tasks *and* takes all the responsibility, leaving you free to be what you want to be. You like pushing the limits in life and then watching the fallout, so when you take this prospective partner to meet the folks (or the kids), you'll stand back with an inner smile and watch their reactions. And there will be one, because you never choose the type of person everyone expects.

All rising signs offer challenges. One of yours is due to your sign being fixed. Fixed signs are stubborn; that seems odd for an air sign. How do you "fix" air? Your fixity and stubbornness reveals itself in your determination to never be anything other than you are. You must be allowed to blow whichever way you want. You will not be changed or moulded by anyone, not even the one you care most about. Partners, children, and the boss can rant and rave all they want—it is water off a duck's back. People find it impossible to negotiate with you because you don't care about the outcome. You cannot be blackmailed or persuaded to anything. You are you: unique, special, and stubborn. You won't budge an inch.

When Aquarius is your rising sign, the main challenge is not to be a maverick just for the sake of it. Your desire to sidestep accepted ways of being could lead to you inadvertently throwing the baby out with the bathwater. Ruled by Uranus, you are always tempted to be different, to be a rulebreaker or to create disruption simply for the sake of it, rather than your real purpose, which is to change out-moded ways of thinking and behaving, to pave the way for a more humanitarian world.

Because of your need for detachment, you observe things from a distance, leading to a wide overview. You absorb many ideas, most of which are bizarre or fringe, and then find you have no idea what to do with them. You are tempted to listen to so many points of view that you lose track of why exactly you are doing it, then you're left wondering what to do with the information you've accu-mulated. In the end, you find you have no idea what your purpose is, and you may decide there is no purpose.

So, what *is* the purpose of Aquarius rising? You are a seer of the future. Being rebellious for the sake of it is a road to nowhere, but if you trust your unique individual-ity and live your life in tune with your own inner compass, you will be grounded in what you know is right, guided by the higher force within, unbiased, non-judgemental, and accepting of all. You are not a seer of the future because you want to be a leader, nor do you have any interest in fame or fortune. You do it because it has to be done, and you are the only sign who can do it. Everyone else is buzz-ing about doing the same old thing, but your vision is light years ahead.

If your sun is in Aquarius as well, you are being given another chance to learn this lesson in this lifetime. This time around, listen to your soul, to that inner voice. Stop trying to be different just because you can or because you find the fallout so hilarious. Then you will see through all the dross to new ways of being, not just for you, but for all of mankind.

Aquarius is the sign of the genius. You are the one who moves past old conditioning, who continually strives for understanding, who revels in the untried and untested. People may not understand that you do not do this for any reward; accolades, success, and material wealth are irrelevant to you. You do this because it is who you are. You are the catalyst for change. Aquarius is the sign of new discoveries and breakthroughs in all fields. The inspiration comes from your innate curiosity that encourages you to test, unveil, and review all known knowledge until you discover the next small step towards enlightenment.

The human race takes small steps forward and over time they add up to a massive leap, and yours is the sign that continually strives to make this happen. You instinctively know that there are vast areas yet to be explored that offer unparalleled knowledge, and you are compelled to search for them. In your own life, this is why you are so detached: you have a higher purpose. You have to be able to follow any breakthrough. You must be free and unfettered in both mind and body to explore our universe.

The lesson for Aquarius rising is to hear those otherworldly messages and allow them to resonate within, because only you can decipher them.

In order to focus your Aquarius energy positively, use the following list as a guide.

1. Pay attention to what is right in front of you now and then, and appreciate what your loved ones are doing for you.
2. Don't choose friends based on their uniqueness, but based on shared ideals.
3. Try not to rock the boat just for the fun of it; other people could get hurt.
4. Be aware of how your words and action impact others, even if it's unintentional.
5. Find a career that utilizes your genius and holds the potential for real breakthroughs.

♓ PISCES: THE OLD SOUL

Your Spiritual Lesson: Keep the needs of others separate from yours, and try to hold on to your inner vision of your own path.

This is the most spiritually rewarding sign to have, but it can certainly be difficult. As mutable water, Pisces's whole being is fluid: ever-flowing, ever-changing, and open to everything in the universe, from the smallest petal of a flower to the vastness of space. In both, and in everything in between, you see a meaning more deep and profound than anyone else. Not that you will be able to verbalize your feelings, unless other aspects in your birth chart suggest otherwise.

Your feelings and intuitions come so fast, and they seem so vivid and true, but then they slip away on the stream of consciousness like a slippery fish you cannot hold in your grasp. By the time you've formed the words to explain something, the whole idea has gone, and you are left with a footprint only, and one slowly melting into wet sand. The print fades but leaves its impression in your mind. Before you can attempt to make sense of it, another feeling appears and the same thing happens, and so your life becomes a constant cycle of impressions, nuances, and intuitions all leaving something behind, but feeling so unreal that you are never sure if you imagined them or not.

Thus, you have a powerful imagination, and an even more powerful intuition. This is an odd word to use for Pisces, *powerful*, but in fact you hold within such a depth of powerful spiritual knowledge that it must dissipate, spreading out like a stream overflowing its bank. Unable to contain the flood, it always flows away, and you float along with it, losing your grip on anything tangible.

Real life (though you don't see it as real in any sense) is a world of excess to you: so much noise, activity, rushing, striving. You shrink from the world because it is so alien to your nature. Nothing about you needs to strive and rush. You alone, of all the zodiac signs, know that you don't have to do anything or go anywhere to learn all that there is to know. True knowledge comes in stillness, peace, and contemplation.

But it is hard not to get involved in a rush of activity because life demands it. So, you try to keep up. You really do. Using the other planets at your disposal, you head out to do what is expected because you also need a roof over your head and food on the table, but each and every day, it is so hard for you to step into the chaos, to function in this world that is so stressful and demanding. It wears you out, and you are easily tired. All those impressions come so thick and fast that they overwhelm you, leaving you confused and floundering. When alone and at peace, you see your true reality, but when you're a part of this chaotic world, you experience so many feelings, thoughts, and noises that it all becomes a jumble. You have no hope of disentangling these impressions and making sense of them before more flood in.

You instinctively know when someone is unhappy, grieving, or lost. Often, you simply sit near them, not saying a word. You may not know it, but you are a healer. It is hard for you to do anything practical for anyone, but you don't need to—your soothing presence is enough. People sense you truly understand their struggles, and even a kindly look or the touch of your hand is balm, though they won't know why. The reason is because you are one of the few people in the world who asks nothing of others, but who still gives their all. When you are balanced and calm, your unconditional love spills out in waves and washes over those who are struggling in life. Thus your soul heals, in silence, with love.

Being so sweet, kind, and helpful, you are prone to being used. People mislead you, hurt you, and tread all over you. Despite your intuition, you may fail to spot someone pulling the wool over your eyes. Often, a stronger partner will attempt to protect you, but in doing so, they have certain demands, and even normal relationship requirements can prove to be too much: shopping, cooking, cleaning, paying bills, setting up the internet, making a phone call, driving, you name it—life is tough.

When life is too busy, you lose your inner compass entirely. So, you escape for your sanity's sake. When everything has gotten to be too much, you get ill, so you call in sick. You may not be sick in the socially accepted sense, but if you don't get some peace and quiet in which to restore your soul, you most certainly will be ill.

Everyday demands are easy for a lot of the other signs. Some may even enjoy it, but not you. Every little thing that isn't based on imagination draws you away from the real you. You have trouble with technical things, and details are anathema to you. All the extraneous paraphernalia of life exhausts you. It requires you to focus a mind that is attuned to otherworldly matters, and you rarely can, so people see you as hopelessly fuzzy, vague, and incapable of dealing with the most mundane of tasks. They see only your failings because they are looking at you in a three-dimensional world and not through the multifaceted truth of your world.

Thus, most Pisces risings need some sort of creative outlet. As a writer, artist, sculptor, musician, or actor, it is often this path to self-expression that saves you. It is so hard to get time to yourself because when you tell people you need some peace, they don't understand you. But with a studio or shed of your own, you can ask not to be disturbed and isolate when life is threatening to undermine you completely. Sometimes you will sit and listen to music; sometimes you write or paint. Regardless, it is the peace you seek, the silence in which to centre yourself, because your soul has been bombarded by so much it has shrunk within itself.

Your sign is the most compassionate, non-judgemental, and loving of the zodiac. You naturally feel the flow of mankind. You know life now is not how it was, nor how it will be; you recognize that we are in a state of continual flux and change. But your rising sign always has its roots in the true essence of life, and in perfect clarity, you can see the meaninglessness of active striving, which brings next to no spiritual enlightenment. Despite your fragility and your prominent consciousness, your roots are firmly in the knowledge of oneness and wholeness. Thus, you are wise and knowing, but you would never presume to preach or explain. It's unlikely you could even if someone asked. That is because you know this knowledge is for you alone. Everyone is on their own spiritual path, and they have their own lessons and their own trials. You wouldn't presume to interfere in a plan so complex and divine. All you want is to freely navigate your own.

These are your lessons: you are not responsible for anyone else. You cannot solve another person's problems, let alone the whole world's, nor are you meant to. Your task is to stay within your own spiritual boundaries and let things flow by without them affecting you. Your rising sign is meant to be in life, but not part of it. The poet Byron said, "I stood among them but not of them; in a shroud of thoughts which were not their thoughts."[1] This line perfectly explains what it is like to have Pisces rising. You must walk amongst people because you have to. You survive the best you can. But all the while, try to remain true to your inner self and keep others' needs separate from yours. Otherwise, they will overwhelm you, and you will lose the true essence of who you are: a soul well along

1. This quote appears in Canto Three, Stanza 113 of Lord Byron's poem "Childe Harold's Pilgrimage," which contains four parts published between 1812 and 1818.

the spiritual path, so much farther along than others that everyday life no longer fulfils you in any way.

Byron wasn't a Pisces rising, but his south node was in the twelfth house, which is the house of Pisces, and the sign there was Gemini, which was why he tried to communicate what it feels like to have a spiritual home in Pisces. He sums it up beautifully: "There is pleasure in the pathless woods, there is rapture in the lonely shore, there is society where none intrudes, by the deep sea, and music in its roar; I love not Man the less, but Nature more."[2]

In order to focus your Pisces energy positively, use the following list as a guide.

1. Endeavour not to take on everyone's problems as your own.

2. Learn how to say no a bit more firmly!

3. It's fine to think of yourself for once.

4. Develop a skill or talent that brings you solace and peace.

5. Choose a career that is laidback yet fulfils your need to be of use.

2. This quote appears in Canto Four, Stanza 178 of Lord Byron's poem "Childe Harold's Pilgrimage," which contains four parts published between 1812 and 1818.

two
The Nodes
and the Houses

Now that you understand how to use your rising sign and its spiritual lessons, let's look at the areas of life you are required to focus on in this lifetime. These are shown in the north and south nodes. The south node is not shown in a birth chart; what is shown are the north nodes. To find the south node, look 180 degrees from the north node.

Nowadays, it is largely accepted that our south node falls in the house (area of life) we inhabited in our past life, and it is an area that makes us feel safe and secure. The idea of the south node being a marker of a past life was first propounded in the middle of the last century by Dane

Rudhyar. His book *The Astrology of Personality* came out in 1936. Other astrologers picked up on this idea, in particular Isabel M. Hickey, who wrote *Astrology: A Cosmic Science* in 1970. By the time my teachers, Bruno and Louise Huber, taught me about the nodes, it was the mid-1980s.

The Hubers believed that the north nodes acted as a pointer to the way personal growth could be achieved in this lifetime, and that the house (area of life) the north node occupied showed individuals their *new* learning task, the opposite of what they were used to (the south node's area of life). They believed that people had to, somehow, try to reach the north node house throughout their lives to balance their experiences.

The idea of the south node inhabiting the house that is our comfort area seems to resonate with everyone. My many years of chart interpretation confirm this—the south node is absolutely a place of comfort for people. It is indeed most likely that we are so familiar with this aspect because of past life experience with it; no other explanation makes any sense.

It also appears true that the north node is our challenge in this life. The Hubers (and many other astrologers) believed that once we accept our life challenge and embrace the north node area of life, we will find inner fulfilment, but my experience has shown that the north node, while certainly a place we are forced to confront at various times and in various ways during our life, is somewhere we are not drawn to at all during the first half of our lives. We move towards the north node with great reluctance and without any conviction, nor any obvious pleasure or joy—unless there is an important planet there as well, by which I mean the sun, moon, Mercury, Venus, or Mars. A planet in our north node house will help us reach it when in previous lives we were unable to, for whatever reason. Regardless, our comfort zone, our place of happiness and contentment, is wherever the south node is located, and we never entirely lose this feeling.

Fortunately, life rarely thrusts us unwillingly into our north node area. We are given opportunities to dip our toe into the waters of the house the north node is in. This way, as we age, we can slowly and gently adjust both our mindset and our focus.

The aim is to balance the two areas by accepting some parts of the north node while utilizing those areas of the south that are intrinsic to who we are. It is this balance that produces happiness and fulfilment, not a complete disregard of the south node, as has been previously suggested. For example, those with a Cancer south node are natural carers. As soon as they can, they start looking after others in a hands-on, empathic way. Their north node will be in Capricorn, which is the career house—an area of little interest in their early years. But, as life progresses, they will learn how to take their innate Cancerian traits across to their north node by accepting that Capricorns also care for family, but financially, not practically. So, their challenge in life is to shift from providing hands-on care to providing financial support. Their task is to develop a particular skill in order to do this, and here lies their true lesson: finding their special skill and using it to help their family by financially supporting them when required. For example, a Cancer south node would still care for their family, but in a different way. Their need to care for others never leaves them, but they find a new way of doing it that also encourages their own growth. It is this pursuit of balancing both nodes that is fulfilling.

The nodes are interpreted firstly by house, then by astrological sign. The houses the two nodes occupy show the areas of life you will have extensive dealings with in this lifetime, and the astrological signs they occupy show you how to go about handling them. In this chapter, I will be discussing the nodes by house.

THE HOUSES

I've talked a lot about the houses and mentioned that they are areas of life, but it might be helpful to explain them in more detail. If you don't yet understand the concept of the houses in astrology, this section should clarify things for you.

Ancient astrologers not only divided the sky into sections based on the constellations (which became the astrological signs), they also divided it into twelve areas that are known as the houses. Each house has a purpose in our lives, so it is necessary to understand what they mean. They are calculated by the time of birth, which sets the chart like a clock; time of birth is incredibly important, and no chart can be considered accurate without it. At your moment of birth, the astrological sign that is rising on the eastern horizon becomes the start of the first house, and all the rest of the houses are calculated from that.

The first six houses at the bottom of the chart—counted counterclockwise from the rising sign—are in what is called the *collective*. This term refers to the people who share the area you grow up in as well as those you frequently encounter in the local environment, perhaps at school, church, the supermarket, or your workplace. The collective, as a whole, shares a similar identity. Usually, a collective believes the same things (taught by family, friends, or schools) and supports each other in many ways. There is a sense of belonging, and of security, in being part of this group.

To understand this concept, think of your chart as a life clock. Each area of life takes six years to traverse, regardless of its size. Starting at the ascendant, you move through the first house (rising sign) until you are six. Then you go through the second house until you are twelve, the third until eighteen, and so on. So these first six houses are activated in the early years of your life, from birth to age thirty-six, which is why they are called the *collective houses*.

When you have important planets in the collective houses (with the exception of those in the first house, which are used to express who you are), they want to be used in the community. So, if your sun is in houses two through six, for example, you'll feel most at home when part of your supportive network.

The other houses, seven to twelve, are at the top part of the chart, and they are considered *individual houses*. That's because these areas of life involve conscious thought and a desire to find our own answers rather than blindly believing what we were told. The individual houses start with the seventh house and correspond to the age of thirty-six upwards. By this point in life, we have often completed our education and found our place in the world. This is the time we start to think for ourselves, which may mean adopting different ideas than the ones we were raised with.

As you progress through the individual houses year by year, you will start developing your own philosophies and talents because you will want to stand out as an individual. You want to make your own decisions about issues and come up with your own answers. Planets here think before acting and don't always accept what they read and hear.

One of your nodes will be in the collective, the other in the individual. This will give you a guide as to the areas of life you should be focusing on in this lifetime, and it will provide a baseline that helps you understand your life challenges more clearly.

Once you've determined your south and north node positions, check out the two houses involved by reading the following brief overview.

FIRST HOUSE:
Appearance and Outward Manner
(And Your Sun Sign in the Previous Life)
Otherwise known as the rising sign or as the ascendant, the first house is ruled by Aries. This house has traditionally been interpreted as how we want the world to see us. Some people say it's how we look, but it is more about how we act—how we behave and the characteristics we outwardly display when first meeting people. As a physical description, it isn't always accurate, though sometimes traits do show through; much will depend on genes, a concept not fully understood when this theory was accepted as fact.

SECOND HOUSE:
Money, Possessions, Personal Talents that Can Be Used to
Make and Maintain a Secure Base, Sense of Self-Worth
This house corresponds to the sign of Taurus, and it is linked to material possessions, money, and security. Any planet here will be concerned with these aspects, and primarily focused on making money. The car we drive, the house we own, and all our acquisitions fall under this house's purview, therefore it also indicates our values: how we see the world and what we want from it. The second

house tends to focus on tangible results achieved with effort. Self-worth is derived from our ability to provide for ourself and others.

THIRD HOUSE:
Education, Learning, Communication, Siblings, Friends, Neighbours, Teachers

This house is the learning/teaching house. It is ruled by Gemini. It encompasses all the people around us: siblings, neighbours, teachers, religious leaders, and those we learn from as we grow. The third house reflects our local community and our collective identity. To use general examples, meeting friends for coffee, going to the sports centre to work out, or shopping locally are third-house activities. This house is concerned with the sort of things we do daily and the people we mix with. It's also the gossipy house and the place of social media.

FOURTH HOUSE:
Family, Home, Nurturing Base

The fourth house encompasses home and family, both the ones we grew up in and the ones we went on to form when we left home. It is ruled by Cancer. The fourth house is your homebase; it is privacy, and the person you are when you close the door to the outside world. It is also concerned with planting roots. Planets here focus on this area.

FIFTH HOUSE:
Self-Expression, Creativity, Children, Love Affairs, Pleasure

This creative house is ruled by Leo. This is the area where we express our individual talents and abilities. It is a tactile house, so it also covers brief love affairs, our attitude towards children, and how we have fun. Planets here show themselves when we are in relaxed settings and using our creative outlets; for example, Mercury in the fifth house will use words as a form of self-expression, likely via writing or acting. The fifth house is the "showiness" behind whatever we do or whatever we create; it fuels our desire for our achievements to be shared/admired by others.

SIXTH HOUSE:
Hands-On Work, Serving Others, Diet and Exercise, Health

This is traditionally called the house of service. It is ruled by Virgo. Planets here focus on helping others. The work undertaken in the sixth house is of the unsung variety, and it is always hands-on. A good example is the day-to-day grind we all have, our daily routine. The other aspect of this house is how we view our health and the steps we take to maintain it (or not). Planets here want to be of practical use in the world.

SEVENTH HOUSE:
Marriage and Long-Term Partnerships

This is the marriage house. Nowadays, fewer people are getting married, so think of the seventh house as reflective of any long-term commitment to a partner, as well as how we view these relationships. Ruled by Venus, the seventh house is where compromises are made to secure harmony, but some planets may use manipulative or controlling means to gain or hang on to partners. In the old days, the seventh house was seen as the place of open enemies; this makes sense, since our nearest and dearest are those we fall out with most often.

EIGHTH HOUSE:
Inheritance, Death, Psychology, What Other People Own/Their Values

The eighth house is concerned with other people: their psychology, values and beliefs, and any money and property they might leave in the form of inheritances. For this reason, it also covers death. This house is ruled by the sign of Scorpio.

NINTH HOUSE:
Private Study Resulting in Individual Philosophy, Teaching at a Higher Level, Seclusion

Ruled by Sagittarius, this is the house of inquisition. It is seen as the thinking house, so it covers higher learning,

teaching at a university level, research, and uncovering esoteric and philosophical truths. Often, this involves travel.
Regardless, the ninth house utilizes both physical movement and mental exploration to discover the truth. Planets
here like to work alone.

TENTH HOUSE:
Career, Status, Being in the Public Eye
The tenth house is the highest part of the chart, so it shows
us the most we can attain in life via our career. It is ruled by
Capricorn, and its focus is on respect, status, and worldly
recognition.

ELEVENTH HOUSE:
Chosen Friendships, Selective Experiences,
Humanitarian Organizations
This is the area of selective friendships and humanitarian aims. This house is ruled by Aquarius. Planets here
want to be with people of like mind; it's where we find our
friends, the groups we've joined, and our ideals.

TWELFTH HOUSE:
Spirituality, Retreat, Isolation
This house is tucked away at the far left-hand side of the
chart. It is ruled by Pisces. The twelfth house is used in a
private, personal way for quiet contemplation in order to
connect with our spiritual beliefs. Any institution removed

from the world is here; think hospitals, prisons, or religious retreats. Anywhere we are alone with our thoughts is twelfth-house territory. It is in stillness that we find our true meaning and purpose.

DETERMINING THE NORTH AND SOUTH NODE

So, where is your south node? If you haven't already created your birth chart, visit an astrology website and type in your time, date, and place of birth.

There are ten planets marked on a chart, but the symbol you are looking for is the one that resembles a headset. This is the north node. Luckily, most sites also provide a list of where your planets are, if you have trouble navigating the image of the chart. Usually, this list includes the north node by house and by sign. You do need to know both to fully understand your purpose, so make a note.

The position of the south node is not marked on a birth chart. You need to either literally or figuratively draw a line directly across the chart from the north node, 180 degrees around the circle. The astrological sign and house opposite the north node is your south node. If you are having trouble determining your south node placement, don't worry too much, because the following sections will tell you where your south node is as long as you know your north node.

The houses are areas of life. If you don't yet understand this concept, go back and reread the previous section. This should make everything clearer. The houses that your south and north node occupy are the areas of life you will have to confront time and again in this lifetime, so understanding what the houses are all about is key to understanding your purpose.

Although the two houses occupied by the north and south nodes are opposite each other, they are on an axis which, according to the Hubers, relate to the areas of life you'll be dealing with in this lifetime. There are six possible axes: the relationship axis, the possession axis, the thinking axis, the individual axis, and the being axis, which involves your beliefs and how you relate to others (friendship).

NODE AXES

This list indicates which axis your north and south node are on.

- If your north node is in the first house, your south node will be in the seventh house. This is the *relationship axis*.
- If your north node is in the second house, your south node will be in the eighth house. This is the *possession axis*.

- If your north node is in the third house, your south node will be in the ninth house. This is the *thinking axis*.

- If your north node is in the fourth house, your south node will be in the tenth house. This is the *individual axis*.

- If your north node is in the fifth house, your south node will be in the eleventh house. This is the *friendship axis*.

- If your north node is in the sixth house, your south node will be in the twelfth house. This is the *being axis*.

- If your north node is in the seventh house, your south node will be in the first house. This is the *relationship axis*.

- If your north node is in the eighth house, your south node will be in the second house. This is the *possession axis*.

- If your north node is in the ninth house, your south node will be in the third house. This is the *thinking axis*.

- If your north node is in the tenth house, your south node will be in the fourth house. This is the *individual axis*.

- If your north node is in the eleventh house, your south node will be in the fifth house. This is the *friendship axis*.
- If your north node is in the twelfth house, your south node will be in the sixth house. This is the *being axis*.

As stated earlier, this chapter focuses on the houses the south and north node occupy. Nodal houses are the areas of life we will consistently encounter in this lifetime. Chapter 3 will explore the astrological signs the north and south node occupy; nodal signs explain the manner in which you can reach your north node, your destiny. Be sure to read both chapters for the most comprehensive understanding of your nodes.

Read the following description that matches your south node's house position, as this is your past life area. As you read, analyse your south node; think long and hard about the aspects of this house and how it makes you feel. Be aware this is your area of security and comfort, and you can retreat here anytime you need to. Think of it as a safe place where you can go to restore your inner balance. Right now, it is more important to focus on the south node as a place you have lived before. You will be guided to your north node throughout life, so there is no need to actively pursue it unless you consciously choose to. But, be aware of it, and when opportunities arise, try to embrace them, because this is your cosmic lesson.

If, in your birth chart, there is a planet in your north node house or sign, you will find it easier to follow your intended path. It's possible you've already had a lifetime (or more than one) and failed to follow your north node, so this time you are being assisted, because a planet in an area draws us there. If a strong planet like the sun or moon is in the same sign or house as your north node, you will find it much easier to achieve your destiny because of the powerful energies these planets exude.

If you have a planet in your south node house, this is telling you that there are some areas of this house that still need to be fully integrated, so you are actively encouraged to balance your north and south nodes by inhabiting both houses (areas of life).

Be aware there is no right or wrong way to work with your nodes. There is never cosmic punishment for not adopting the aspects of your north node—the universe is supportive, not unkind. You will find that you naturally move in the direction of your north node as life progresses and that, over time, it will not appear as uninviting as it once did.

SOUTH NODE FIRST HOUSE ➡ NORTH NODE SEVENTH HOUSE

Comfort Zones: Using your own talents and abilities; being independent, capable, and confident

Challenges: Learning to compromise; creating balance and fairness; forming harmonious partnerships

RELATIONSHIP AXIS

The relationship axis is all about how we relate to others. The first house is on the left-hand side of the chart, and planets here are used solely by you, because energies are not shared with others in this house. This house is about who you are and how you express your individual identity. The seventh house, which is exactly opposite on the right-hand side of the chart, directs planetary energy towards other people, and the compromise you need to make in this lifetime is to live in harmony with others.

YOUR LAST LIFE: YOUR SOUTH NODE

The first house is ruled by the sign of Aries. Being the first sign of the zodiac, Aries is the child in astrological terms, and children are very me-focused and self-centred, aware of only their needs, and this accurately describes the energy of the first house. This south node position means you spent your last lifetime (or lifetimes) learning all about yourself. To do so meant always putting yourself and your needs first. It was all about *you*.

We are taught that we should be considerate of the feelings of others, and of course this is just, but this position indicates that in your last life, you were given permission to be self-absorbed. That's because when we give of ourselves, when we compromise with people, and when we consider the needs of others first and foremost, we tend to lose our own identity.

Having spent time in this house in previous lives, it will be natural for you to be independent, capable, and driven, answering to no one. That doesn't mean you are selfish or unkind—it means you are focused on outcomes.

In the last life, you discovered your own strengths and weaknesses. You learnt all about how to start new things, to forge new pathways, to be the leader, the initiator, and the one who suggested new directions.

The ram is the symbol of this sign and house, and rams don't think, they do. You learnt that obstacles were best overcome with brute force. An obstacle was seen as a challenge. How quickly could you overcome it? Not for one second did you see obstacles as learning experiences or warnings. In fact, warnings spurred you on. There was nothing you loved more than proving people wrong when they suggested caution. Rather than hesitate, you rose to the challenge of proving yourself. In truth, you detested people warning you. Your inner confidence was often enough to topple any obstacle. You developed the mindset that you could—and would—deal with every difficulty.

You probably lived alone, but if not, you still acted independently. Relationships take patience and compromise and you had neither, nor were they required of you.

THIS LIFETIME: YOUR NORTH NODE

Because of the memory of your past life, everything you do now is infused with an inner certainty of who you are and your sense of self-worth. You don't ask anyone to do what you don't do yourself; in fact, you prefer to do things yourself, because you know you can rely on yourself to get things done, and quickly! You really hate waiting on others.

In your past life, you knew your own strengths. Now, this gives you the courage to be yourself, to say what you think and do what you want. Others will both admire you for this and loathe your lack of consideration, but this is the true you. You do, in fact, do wonderful things for others, but you must do it in your way and in your own time. You cannot adhere to others' schedules or sit idly by when an idea comes to you.

Action is important to you. You might drive an ambulance, save someone from a burning building, start the ball rolling to get a new hospital or school built, or demand extra funding in your blunt, no-nonsense way, but you probably won't be the one teaching or nursing. You forge new pathways, sweep away red tape, demand answers, fight for change, and begin projects. To expect you to pussyfoot around people—to be kind, considerate, and compromising—is not in line with your role. You feel you are a warrior, a leader, and an innovator.

This is your comfort zone now, this knowledge of who you are. You can stand alone and work alone, and you are capable and sure of yourself. When life gets tough, you know you can rely on yourself to manage. You honestly don't need other people at all. You feel safer relying on your own resources; you trust only yourself. You are truly independent.

Your balance in this life is to learn all about relationships and how to compromise. This will be a very hard task for you. The north node is in the sign of partnerships and peaceful co-operation, and this is an area you feel reluctant to pursue. Allowing someone else to make decisions? Waiting for someone patiently? Putting your partner first? How are you supposed to do that when you prefer being the independent, capable, and proactive person you are? It feels impossible and uncomfortable—very uncomfortable. How can you trust someone else when you know you don't need them?

The universe is not asking you to go against your inner being, but it is asking you to have a go at compromise. You can always step back to your comfort zone, can't you? No one can take your inner security away from you. It is who you are, and you are proud to be independent. But you are destined to meet someone who makes you stop and think. To keep this special someone in your life, you will need to temper your me-first attitude or you may risk losing them. Thus, you will try to make adjustments and compromises. That is all this position is asking of you. It isn't expecting you to suddenly become a doormat who gives in to everything your partner asks. The universe is simply asking you to try and understand another's point of view.

Think about these two areas of life. It is not ideal to be so independent that you don't need others, nor do you want to be so needy that you lose who you are. These nodes are advising you to balance things out. Give personal relationships a chance. Try to let go of your ego to allow a significant other some room in your life. You may find you enjoy letting someone else make the decisions for a change.

Knowing that you are truly independent and cannot help being that way because of your past life is liberating, both for you and your future long-term partner. You now understand the inner drive you have to be on your own and why you find relationships so challenging, and if you accept this about yourself—and, in turn, explain it to your partner—you have a better chance of developing a meaningful partnership. Success will also will depend on how understanding and accepting your partner is; are they prepared to work with you to resolve any relationship difficulties?

This is why astrology is so mind-opening. No longer are you operating in the dark. The problem area is "out there," acknowledged and accepted, and it can be worked on by both of you. Make it a game full of humour; life doesn't have to be serious. Allow your partner to point out when you are getting overly bossy, and admit with good grace that yep, you are, but that you do it because it's natural and because you love them and want to protect them. Laugh about it, but then make more of an effort to not sound so bossy. It's a win-win situation. However, if you don't dig deeper into your motives, your "I don't need anyone" attitude could break up the relationship.

It is not just your relationship with partners that will require a more compromising attitude. Throughout your life, there will be times when you will be called to step back and allow someone else to take charge. There will be situations in which you will be forced to compromise: in relationships, in the workplace, and in your dealings with people. Be aware you only have to take baby steps, to *try* to be more compromising and attentive. You do not always have to be the first to rush in; wait for others. Accept that another's point of view is just as valid as yours. Astrology is key to understanding your life purpose and why you act as you do. Understanding your nodes will make your own life easier, and your relationships—absolutely all of them—will benefit from this self-awareness.

> ### SOUTH NODE SECOND HOUSE ➡ NORTH NODE EIGHTH HOUSE
>
> **Comfort Zones:** *Obtaining possessions through hard work; building security; standing on your own two feet*
> **Challenges:** *Relying on other people; accepting another's values and beliefs; sublimating yourself for another*

POSSESSION AXIS

This second house/eighth house axis is called the possession axis because it is all about what you own and what other people own. A whole gamut of experiences can be generated by this nodal combination, from being totally independent financially to being totally *dependent* financially.

YOUR LAST LIFE: YOUR SOUTH NODE

In the last life, you lived mostly in the second house, ruled by Taurus. This house focuses on financial gain and security through possessions, so working hard and building security were your top priority. You would have taken care of others who couldn't work because of their age, gender, or an incapacity that prevented them from supporting themselves. You became used to keeping your eye on the finances and looking after others. You embodied the characteristics of a hard-working, financially minded business person, someone who shouldered the burdens of those you loved. You would have made sure everyone was well provided for and safe.

Make no mistake, we all seek financial security. It is not a bad thing to want to be secure. Only a few decades back, there was no safety net in the form of pensions as there is today. Most people worked until they simply couldn't, and then they hoped their family would care for them. You wouldn't have minded working long hours and doing it all on behalf of others. You intrinsically understood you had stamina, staying power, inner strength, and purpose and drive, and because of that, you should look after those who were weaker or more vulnerable. Your whole life was one of steady, uncomplaining, patient service, with a focus on money.

The second house is all about standing on your own two feet in life and providing for yourself and any dependents, and you did this well in the last life. You proved you could stand alone and be responsible, and you developed this stable, steady, hard-working, independent nature as your life progressed. It is likely you ended up with considerable wealth, or at the very least, comfortably off.

With this comes a downside: you may have considered others your possessions, too. It can be a slippery slope to take financial responsibility for someone else; it is easy to slip into thinking that you then have control of that person, that you "own" them. This is why the second/eighth house axis is called the possession axis: it's not just about what you own, but *who* you feel you own.

Because the second house is concerned with money, there is also a danger of placing too much emphasis on money, creating the false belief that there is never enough and that no matter how hard you work, the rewards aren't commensurate. It's easy to fall into a mindset that places too much importance on material possessions, and you may have begun to base your self-worth on how much you earn, the house you own, and the car you drive. This creates a never-ending cycle of working even harder to keep up with everyone else—because there will always be someone with a better salary, house, and car.

Another possibility is becoming overly afraid of losing what you do have, which can spark a miserly, greedy, or suspicious frame of mind. These are the danger areas when money is involved. However, this nodal placement does not guarantee you were in any way like this in the past; rather, this is a possibility when too many lifetimes focus on one area, hence the need to balance our south node with its opposite in our current lifetime.

THIS LIFETIME: YOUR NORTH NODE

Because the second house is your comfort area in this life, you have intrinsically adopted a financially motivated mindset. You found a job as soon as you could and began accumulating money and possessions. It's likely you are already creating wealth and abundance through your own efforts. The second house south node is least likely to get sidetracked, for you don't want to be beholden to anyone else.

But you've already proven you can be financially secure. In this lifetime, you will be asked to balance this money-focused and independent nature by accepting help from others. This will really go against your morals, because you know how capable you are. But you must learn to balance being responsible for yourself and allowing others to care for you. Bear in mind, business or romantic partners may be learning the opposite lesson: how to stand on their own two feet and be financially responsible, when in the past they were protected and looked after; you may be in a mutual learning process in this life, swapping roles in effect. It's uncanny how many couples have opposite nodal positions.

When someone is in control financially, their values and beliefs are often accepted. The power dynamic shifts. If someone is paying the bills, supporting a university student, or providing a loan to a business, they expect a certain amount of respect, and they will be given it. Remember that old phrase "money talks." The one who pays the bills sets the tone, in effect. Because you were the one who had the power in your last life, your mindset will need some readjustment in this lifetime. Not only will you be required to graciously accept offerings from others, you will have to adapt your own opinions to bring them into alignment with theirs. This is not to say you must give up work, lounge around, change your allegiances for someone else. In truth, being wholly dependent on someone else is not something you can bring yourself to do. Instead, you must view life as a give-and-take affair.

Throughout your life, opportunities will present themselves that give you a chance to allow someone else to take financial responsibilities off your shoulders. You will probably resist. One way or another, there will come a moment when the rug might be pulled out from under you, and you may find yourself unable to provide for yourself the way you would like. It might be an illness, but more than likely, your career choice won't pan out or the financial markets will fail. There are any number of ways you might find yourself not able to be the sole provider. It will then be necessary for you to graciously accept assistance from someone, no matter how difficult you find it.

Life is not expecting you to give up all your hard-earned possessions. It is asking you to try, now and then, to accept something from someone else. Accept with an honest and heartfelt thank you, and you might find that you both manage to balance your finances in a mutually rewarding way, both giving and receiving. You will never be anything but that independent, capable person at heart, but life is all about learning, and this is your task when the north node is in the eighth house.

Traditionally, the eighth house is concerned with inheritance and death; what we get from others when they die, in effect. Some people who are strongly second-house oriented do think about how much money they might obtain when a well-to-do family member dies. This money axis is fraught with dangers.

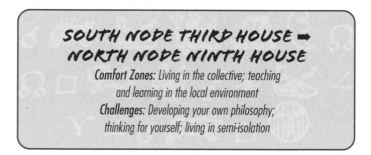

SOUTH NODE THIRD HOUSE ➡ NORTH NODE NINTH HOUSE

Comfort Zones: *Living in the collective; teaching and learning in the local environment*
Challenges: *Developing your own philosophy; thinking for yourself; living in semi-isolation*

THINKING AXIS

The thinking axis deals with the two areas of a chart concerned with how we process and communicate. At one end of the scale are learning by rote, abiding by the status quo, and accepting common beliefs without question. At the other end is the desire to think for ourselves and make up our own mind about everything, from religious beliefs to the political issues of the day.

YOUR LAST LIFE: YOUR SOUTH NODE

Your comfort zone, the area you feel most at home, is the third house. Because this is the house of early education and learning, speech, writing, and communication, these are things you are comfortable with. It is likely you were a teacher or educator in the last life, and this type of job will be second nature to you—so appealing, in fact, that you may even seek to teach again this time.

The third house is at the bottom of the chart in the area called the collective. All six houses at the bottom of the chart have to do with finding our place in the world as we grow, and this third house covers neighbours, siblings, education up to university level, and the local community. This means your main focus in the last life was on the people around you. You would have made a strong contribution to your neighbourhood and the people close to you.

You learnt to effortlessly form links with people. It's likely you had a lot of friends and acquaintances as well as a very active life. You enjoyed being busy and on the move all day, especially in your local community. The idea of upping sticks to another area would not have appealed to you. You had many local connections, and you wanted to keep them because they made you feel secure.

This south node and its opposite north node are all about communication and thought. At the bottom of the chart, your south node was focused on education up to the university level, where knowledge is learnt through memorization, very often the same knowledge that has been taught ever since schooling began: how to read and write, the basics of subjects like history and geography, everyday math. So, in your last life, the way you thought about things was influenced by the way everyone else thought, and you rarely formed your own ideas. Intrinsically, you believed that what you were told by your teachers and educators was correct. After all, they were older adults in a position of authority. In addition, the things you were told by your parents and siblings was accepted as the norm and formed the basis of your knowledge. You didn't question what they said because you naturally assumed they knew what they were talking about.

When you now teach or communicate in any way, you do so using the same framework of knowledge. Because the third house is your comfort zone, this is where you will seek to stay. In your community, you know your place, understand your role, and feel comfortable exchanging information that is accepted by everyone. It will come naturally to help out where you can, to teach, to do volunteer work, and to work close to home in any sphere that has education or communication at its core.

THIS LIFETIME: YOUR NORTH NODE

The opposite house, the one you will be asked to have dealings with in this life, will be a place you do not want to go. That's because it is isolated from the community. The ninth house is all about private study. It is about being alone to do research. It is about individual thinking; a conscious personal search for the meaning of life, or at the very least, trying to find new ways of expressing old ideas.

Your north node is asking you not to accept everything you are told, but to question it, and to find your own answers to the big questions: Who am I, what am I doing here, what is life about, what is my role, and why? It is asking you to dig deeper to find better ways of imparting information about a subject close to your heart, or new insights regarding it. The north node is indicating you have just as much right to propound a new view as anyone else.

To be able to do this will require quiet study. It will require isolation in which to think. It will require stepping back from the busy collective and endeavouring to see life from a more objective perspective. It means recognizing that collective knowledge is not the only truth, or the ultimate truth. You are being asked to develop your own philosophy based on your research instead of relying on what you were told by others, no matter how highly you value their opinions. People with an emphasis on the third house are those most likely to believe everything they see in the news and to accept everyone's ideas as fact. You must try to be more discerning; not everything you are told is true simply because that's what has always been taught.

You are being asked to look beneath the surface for hidden motives. For example, if a respected academic submits a new theory, you generally will not question it, but rather accept it as fact. However, look deeper. The theory could be erroneous. Maybe they are seeking a name for themselves or are after money, so they have cut corners. Your naiveté is lovely, because you are trusting; if someone sounds confident, you believe them. But with this nodal axis, you are being asked to think more deeply about everything you hear and read, and to judge for yourself.

The ninth house covers esoteric subjects, higher learning, seeking the truth (of any subject, be it engineering or astrology), exploring other cultures, studying ancient histories, learning languages, and travelling to far-flung places to unearth new mysteries. Accordingly, all of these descriptions fall under the umbrella of the ninth house: television presenters who visit foreign peoples to show how they live, historians who educate us as to the ancient past of foreign civilizations, missionaries, religious leaders who seek to provide their own version of the truth, lecturers who teach subjects at a high level, astrologers, and those who study esoteric subjects.

The scene often used to describe the feel of the ninth house is a professor alone in a study, at a desk, writing papers or books on a specific field of research. The professor dips in and out of teaching occasionally, but when the professor does teach, it is only to those above the age of eighteen. Whereas the third-house teacher may teach children, the ninth-house professor lectures to adults. Can you see how these two houses are opposites, and what is being asked of you?

You were such a sociable person in the last life, so busy and active, that the mere idea of solitude is scary. To be alone, to live alone, to work alone, to study alone—you really don't like those ideas. You prefer being out and about. Lockdown must have provided many challenges for you if you worked from home; no doubt you took every opportunity to connect with people online. Without that daily interplay, you feel your life is without meaning.

It's likely you automatically slotted into a third-house lifestyle this time around and became a teacher or assumed an important role in your local community. You are drawn to fields with communication at their core—that's your comfort zone, after all, and comes naturally. The world is not asking you to become someone totally alien. All that is being asked is that you open your mind to the fact that there are answers to questions that you alone can find, and that you might actually enjoy the intellectual challenge this presents. In other words, you can still be an educator, but choose a subject that is different, or find a new way of teaching an old subject to balance both of your nodes. Think outside the box instead of being led by past beliefs.

You will come to realize during this life that the knowledge within the collective is not necessarily the truth you believed it to be. You will begin to see you need your own philosophy to bridge this gap, otherwise you will feel rudderless. You will slowly start to open your eyes to greater possibilities.

In the meantime, the collective is always there, ready to offer its support. But by the time you retire from the working world, it's a pretty sure bet that you will have developed a wider view and a more personal philosophy—and you might even enjoy being on your own now and then, just to think.

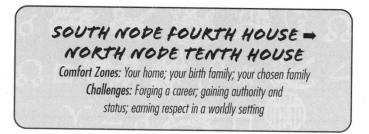

SOUTH NODE FOURTH HOUSE ➡ NORTH NODE TENTH HOUSE
Comfort Zones: Your home; your birth family; your chosen family
Challenges: Forging a career; gaining authority and status; earning respect in a worldly setting

INDIVIDUAL AXIS

The two houses that are on the individual axis have to do with the home/family and career. So, why is this called the individual axis? Because when we are young, we naturally adopt our birth family's beliefs and values. But as life progresses, we begin to see things slightly differently; we may decide we don't think the same way as our parents do. This process can only occur when we venture into the world and meet new people, and it is usually via our career that we are confronted with aims, ideals, and views that are totally at variance with those we grew up with. We make adjustments, keep some of our old beliefs, and discard others, thus becoming an individual.

YOUR LAST LIFE: YOUR SOUTH NODE

This south node is in the fourth house (area of life) that represents your home: the area you grew up in, your birth family (or the people who formed your family), and the shared heritage that gave you emotional and practical security as you grew up. Because of your south node's position, the place you feel most at home *is* your home. Home is important to all of us, but for you, it has an even deeper significance. This nurturing base is essential to your well-being.

As soon as you are old enough, you will be motivated to create your own home because of its particular importance to you. This overriding desire can result in rushing into a serious relationship with someone convenient rather than waiting and being more selective. That is not to say the relationship won't work—it might. You, more than anyone else, will tolerate a great deal rather than lose this family base; because having your own family means so much to you, there is a deep fear that you won't find anyone else who wants to settle down with you. Whatever happens to any household you form, you will keep trying until you have the family unit that provides the nurturing and support that is so necessary for you. Only when you have that secure base do you feel able to venture into the world.

At your core, you need this familial sense of belonging. This fourth house is at the bottom of the chart and represents your roots, and nothing is more necessary than a connection to our roots. Even those without this south node placement use the home as a secure base and a place to return to nurturance. But for you, the fourth house goes far deeper—it is central to being a functioning individual.

So, your last life's focus was the family unit. This axis does not explain if it was a happy or sad experience, only that family had a deep significance to you. The fourth house is a place of depth. Everyone, without exception, has feelings about their childhood home, even if those feelings are negative. The home is never a blank area. In other words, this house carries many and varied emotions and experiences that resonate throughout the rest of our lives. But it is a subjective area. Every child within the same family has different memories of it, and when questioned, has dissimilar experiences and reflections.

In this life, those who are lucky enough to have had a supportive, nurturing family usually go on to do well for themselves. When the south node is here, your childhood was usually a positive experience, or else you wouldn't feel the need to recreate it. All you are, and all you can be, emanates from this base, and without it you feel lost at sea. You can do nothing until you have this perceived security. The downside of this is that you may feel tied to home by necessity, so you might not explore all the possibilities available to you in life. Or, as mentioned earlier, you may tolerate a less-than-perfect partner or family structure rather than walking away and starting again.

THIS LIFETIME: YOUR NORTH NODE

Your north node in this life is in the tenth house, which is the career house. But this does not represent just any old career: jobs fall under the sixth house, so anything in the tenth is visible to the world, a bit more high-profile. You may have to give presentations or train others, or perhaps you are a spokesperson. Ideally, you will be your own boss. This house sits right at the top of the chart and shows the very best you can be in society, the pinnacle of your worldly success. But, when the south node is in the fourth house, a high-profile career will not be of any interest. You may not mind hard work, but have no desire to stand head and shoulders above everyone else. You are quite content to do your work and then return to your nurturing, comfortable home.

With these nodal placements, you aren't being asked to abandon your home, but you are being asked to aim as high as you can in your career. Develop your talents and abilities and share them with the world. If you have a planet in the tenth house, this will be easier for you. Also keep in mind that people with this nodal position prefer to work from home in order to balance these two areas of life.

The tenth house is not just about being the boss. It is the area you reach when you really have something to offer the world based on your own experience and knowledge. It is rarely attained when young, requiring a lifetime of striving to be the very best in your chosen field. Each and every obstacle you encounter will challenge you to do better, to grow, and to find a way through. This wisdom of the tenth house is only gained after a lifetime of experience, which is why those who succeed here are revered and admired. This house has nothing to do with glamour or a quick buck, and everything to do with respect for someone whose experience and expertise develops into an authority born of many years of hard work. This is the ideal to aim for when the north node is in the tenth house.

In this life, your home and family will provide the necessary succour and support that enables you to venture forth into the world. With a supportive family, you know you can aim high, for you will always be caught by the safety net that is your home. This may sound easy, but for some reason, these nodes are more challenging than all the others.

The fourth house is right at the bottom of the chart, and it represents your roots. The tenth house is right at the top, and it shows the highest point you can reach in the outside world: how successful you can be in your career, and how your decisions affect others. Think of it as standing tall with your feet firmly rooted in the fourth and your head up in the tenth. In this life, you will be forced to confront the tenth house via your career, but as soon as you strive to become an individual and move up from the collective family unit, you will begin to question if the values your birth family had align with you now that you are an adult. To figure this out often requires a temporary separation from them. It is possible that this will happen when you form your own family, or perhaps you will be required to work in another part of the country, or another country altogether. In some way, there will come a point when you must assess what you feel is the right way to live.

You will need time and space to consider your own values, to discover if they are in alignment with those you were taught as you grew up, or if you feel differently about things. Your connection to your roots is so strong that it will be hard to separate your thoughts and beliefs from your family's. In effect, in this life, you must strive to find yourself as an *individual*, not as part of a unit, no matter how caring and supportive that unit may have been.

SOUTH NODE FIFTH HOUSE ➡ NORTH NODE ELEVENTH HOUSE

Comfort Zones: Expressing your creativity; impulsive behaviour; love affairs; children
Challenges: Being more selective of your friendships and relationships; developing humanitarian aims

FRIENDSHIP AXIS

This is called the friendship axis because the two houses involved are concerned with friendships, both those we have as we grow (generally, acquaintances who come and go and whom we rarely judge) and the friendships we form when older, when we are more selective. These friendships are typically with people who share our ideals and are of a like mind.

YOUR LAST LIFE: YOUR SOUTH NODE

Your south node area, the fifth house, is at the bottom of the chart. This area is part of the collective, so you feel most at home when you are in your local environment rubbing shoulders with everyone. You have a natural affinity for creating connections. These contacts will be based on friendship and romance, but the links here are transient; the people you connect with here are "here today, gone tomorrow."

Your previous existence would have been spent in the fifth-house area of self-expression. You were likely the life and soul of the party. At a bar, you met and mingled with everyone, developing brief liaisons and living in the moment. Actors, musicians, and artists all fall under this house, as does anyone in the medical profession because they often have to touch complete strangers in an intimate way. This is a good example of how fleeting, yet personal, the interactions are in the fifth house.

When your south node is here, you spent the last life honing all aspects of your creative and interpersonal skills, so it's highly likely you had an innate talent in some creative area—maybe as that artist, writer, sculptor, actor, or musician previously mentioned? Or perhaps you worked in a medical field? Regardless, your life was full of self-expression. Children also fall under the umbrella of this house; there is nothing more self-expressive than having a child. So, working with children or entertaining children are also expressions of the fifth house. People with this south node may be tempted to have a large family.

Love affairs are also under the purview of the fifth house. You come into this life with an easy approach to romance. You will be adept at forming brief relationships, as you know exactly how to attract others. You are prone to having many partners throughout your life. Most likely, you have been supremely confident from an early age. You head straight over to someone you want to be in a relationship with, and you instinctively know exactly the right things to say and how to behave in order to get a date. This confidence is incredibly appealing to the person you approach—so appealing, in fact, that you often succeed where others have failed. The rest of us wonder how you do it! Well, chances are it's because of the past-life experiences that made you so adept at romantic interactions. You come into this life with an inner confidence in who you are and how you express yourself.

When your south node is in the fifth house, down in the collective, you function really well in crowds and may feel at home in bawdy atmospheres; no amount of rough or lewd behaviour fazes you; you can handle it. You enjoy the rough-and-tumble of ordinary life and are not afraid to interact with everyone, even the most unpopular in the community. Plus, you see nothing wrong with expressing yourself in whatever way you like. You have no moral shame (in the nicest sense) and simply follow your instincts without considering how your behaviour might be viewed by others. In fact, you feel more at home with ordinary people than those with airs and graces, and you can handle yourself very well using your natural charm, humour, and charisma to diffuse any tense situations.

THIS LIFETIME: YOUR NORTH NODE

In this life, your north node—your learning curve, your life lesson—is in the eleventh house. Life is not asking you to leap straight from one value system to another, but to give it a try. So, what is the eleventh house all about? Well, it is the polar opposite of the fifth house.

In the eleventh house, you start to think about the people you meet and their behaviour from an objective viewpoint. This house is calm, logical, and detached. It is not a tactile house; it is a place of reasoning and discernment. In this life, you are to stop having random encounters, to halt the physical self-expression that comes so naturally to you, and to start *thinking* about the experiences you have. The eleventh is an intellectual house, not a physical house.

With this north node, you are to be very selective of your friends and acquaintances. You should be careful about who you mix with and certainly do not want to be down at the bar mingling with just anyone. The eleventh house is at the top of the chart in a position of "looking down" on the impulsive, instinctive behaviour of others. A lot of thought goes into who you have as friends. You choose people with whom you have shared interests. Personal relationships are judged from the same standpoint, so they become less frequent and more considered.

In this life, your experiences will draw you (probably reluctantly at first) into this rarefied atmosphere where people make judgements about the whole human race; these decisions form the basis for laws and political movements, for humanitarian actions and even personal actions to improve man's lot. As you get older, you'll find a lot of that early confidence waning, and you will be disinclined to be in a relationship with someone you don't have anything in common with. This applies to your friendships too. You will be more selective of *everyone* who becomes a part of your life.

Those with an emphasis in eleventh are choosy. Their partners have to live up to their high standards. Often even family is kept at arm's length. I'm sure we know someone in our family who attends get-togethers but never appears as committed or involved, who sits slightly apart from everyone. While they are friendly, they are also detached. They will be careful of who they interact with and may even appear "snobbish." This is a good illustration of the eleventh house in an ordinary, everyday setting.

In this life, you are being asked to try and reach the eleventh, so one way or another, you will be required to separate yourself from the collective and enjoy the company of a group of people who have high standards for their fellow man. Always, though, you will long to be down in the collective, because that is your comfort zone. It might be possible to combine the two areas by using your past-life experience and invaluable knowledge in a manner that helps those in the collective.

SOUTH NODE SIXTH HOUSE ➡ NORTH NODE TWELFTH HOUSE

Comfort Zones: *Hard work; service; duty; attention to health*
Challenges: *To just "be"; meditation; spiritual search*

BEING AXIS

The sixth house is all about existence—basically, survival. This is the house (area of life) where everyone learns to use their talents and abilities in a practical and useful way. We all need a roof over our heads and food on the table, so we have to find a way of developing our talents and using them constructively in the world. It is here we roll up our sleeves and get on with real service. The work here in the sixth is hands-on physical labour.

The opposite house, the twelfth, is all about finding what the meaning of life is *for you*. This involves long periods of quiet meditation and reflection, so it suggests a life of retreat and isolation, or at least a lot of time spent alone. It is a perfect opposite in the sense that no physical work at all is required, just a lot of thoughtful contemplation. This requires stepping off the carousel of life and being a bystander, something those used to the sixth house find it incredibly hard to do.

YOUR LAST LIFE: YOUR SOUTH NODE

If your south node is in the sixth house, you come into this existence with a natural, innate feeling that you are called on to be of use to people. If you look at the psychology of it, life is an exchange. In return for work, you receive rewards. In the last life, you became adept at this and never shirked a duty or a responsibility. Service is now as natural to you as breathing. If someone wants help, you automatically offer your services. Working hard is not a problem, and you won't mind how menial a task is; if something needs to be done, you will do it.

The innate danger here is becoming a martyr. Because it is so instinctive for you to be of use, you often don't know where to draw the line between being helpful and becoming a doormat. It is easy for you to over-work in an effort to be all things to all people, then feel aggrieved that people are taking advantage of you (which some will, of course).

Working too hard and losing a work/life balance is also a danger zone with this south node. This can result in illness, either physical or mental. The trouble is, you see the work that needs to be done and can't help but try to fix things. But the work is never-ending. There is an old expression: "Work will be there when you are not." You should repeat this to yourself daily; otherwise, you may become little more than a servant to others, and be exploited by them.

If your south node is in this house, you now have a good appreciation of your talents and how to use them to gain security in this life. Hard work is not a problem for you. This is your comfort zone, so you certainly feel better when being of use. It is hard for you to sit about doing nothing. But, in this life, you will be asked to consider other options. This is offered to you in the twelfth house.

THIS LIFETIME: YOUR NORTH NODE

Your task is to aim for the twelfth house, but what is the twelfth house all about? For a start, it is the polar opposite of the sixth house. The twelfth house is tucked away on the far left of the chart and is the place of spiritual development. In this house, nothing is being asked of you in the physical world. You are being allowed to live quietly, alone, in order to contemplate your reason for existence, to find out who you are and what your spiritual needs are. It is a place where you search for a higher consciousness. In effect, it's an area of retreat, of isolation, of being alone to meditate.

The reason these two houses are connected is that if you over-work in the sixth house (or believe you are indispensable and exhaust yourself in the service of others), you can become ill. When ill, you may end up hospitalised to heal physically or mentally—or, sometimes, both. And any place that is removed from the bustle of life, where we stop and just "be," is considered a twelfth-house area. Hospitals are twelfth-house areas, as are prisons. Those who cannot find an outlet for their skills and abilities or who struggle to develop them may turn to crime to get what they want, which results in similar isolation. Religious retreats are also twelfth-house areas, and even being alone in your own home with a lot of time to think is twelfth-house energy. In effect, the twelfth house is embodied in any place that allows you time away from the busy world in order to find yourself and to discover what you believe.

The ideal path to the twelfth house is to consciously allow yourself time away from work in which to think, preferably on your own. In silence and stillness come inspiration, knowledge, and wisdom. This house is a deeply introspective place. Giving yourself time to meditate will allow space for nuances and intuitions you've been too busy to notice.

Because of your south node, it's highly likely that this will not appeal to you at all. You might not actually like being alone, and you rarely allow yourself time to think or to sit and do nothing; you always find things to do. This hard work of the sixth house is your comfort area, but your task in this lifetime is to take every opportunity to develop the twelfth-house area of your life. Often, as life progresses, you will be offered ways to do this. If you refuse, life will find a way of making time for you to pursue the twelfth house—through illness, or maybe losing your job, or perhaps discovering that people don't need you as much anymore. We all retire from work eventually, and if you retire and still have not taken time to discover the twelfth house, that's a good time to start.

Nothing is being asked of you in the twelfth house. You gave yourself fully in the last life. In a way, the twelfth house north node is a reward, but you won't see it like that, not for a long while. This is the house of non-judgemental and universal love. Only here, in this isolation from the world, can you look to your own spiritual development. In this life, you are being asked to understand the whole as an objective observer, and to draw your own conclusions about who you are and what your spiritual purpose is. Your challenge in life is to develop your spiritual side in solitary contemplation.

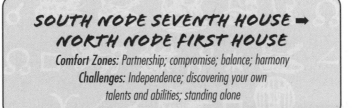

SOUTH NODE SEVENTH HOUSE ➡ NORTH NODE FIRST HOUSE

Comfort Zones: *Partnership; compromise; balance; harmony*
Challenges: *Independence; discovering your own talents and abilities; standing alone*

RELATIONSHIP AXIS

This connection between the seventh house and the first house is all about the deep and meaningful relationships we create (or avoid) in our life. If you have these nodal positions, your challenge and learning curve in this life is on the relationship axis. Your life lessons are all about this area of your existence: marriage and long-term relationships versus being alone.

YOUR LAST LIFE: YOUR SOUTH NODE

With the south node in the seventh house, you learnt all about how to maintain a long-term partnership with someone in your last life. As we know, this involves a lot of compromise, tolerance, understanding, and acceptance. It was also necessary to be supportive, constructive, and willing to contribute to the unit. You learnt all these things and put others first many a time.

The seventh house is ruled by Venus, which creates the desire for a peaceful and harmonious life. This planet encourages and supports our efforts to balance our needs with another's to create a good relationship that can stand the test of time. To do this required you to share your needs and desires with your partner, and in return, you listened patiently to theirs. Together, you learnt how to best fulfil your individual roles within the joint unit. With this south node, you would have been required to sublimate your own wishes and needs at times. You did this to maintain harmony and peace in the relationship.

Because you spent your last life developing these skills, you came into this life well-equipped to form fulfilling relationships. You know how to maintain harmony. You learnt that a long-term partnership can be likened to two horses in harness, both equally sharing the burdens of life (children, elderly parents, housework, illness, financial responsibility, etc.). The most successful relationships are those where both parties equally pull their weight.

It is likely that in this life, you formed a relationship as soon as you were old enough to do so, and you probably settled down fairly quickly because it felt so right. The seventh house is your comfort zone, so you are happier when in a pair. You have no trouble adapting to another person in order to make a relationship work.

This can create its own problems, though. Perhaps you are too obliging. Have you sublimated yourself to the point where you only relate to yourself as half of a unit? Have you lost sense of who you are as an individual? Most of know at least one couple who had been together for many years that, when separated by death or divorce, became completely lost and rudderless on their own, struggling to establish their individuality again.

You have no problem at all when in partnership with others, romantic or otherwise. You naturally function at your best when with another. After all, Venus is the planet of love, and this is as natural to you as breathing.

THIS LIFETIME: YOUR NORTH NODE

Who are you as an individual? Do you know? This is the challenge inherent in this north node. In this life, you will be asked to answer that question. Even though you will naturally seek out partnerships, life will find ways of presenting opportunities for you to explore who you are as an individual. Perhaps your partner will find themselves unable to participate in day-to-day life due to illness, or works away from home for periods of time, or has a job that means they work long hours. Or maybe, through no fault of your own, your relationships fail. (You may be good at them, but others may still be learning.)

In one way or another, you will find yourself falling back on your own resources and being forced into individualism. The place of individual development is at the far left of the chart, in the first house. This is where you develop your coping mechanisms for functioning alone. In effect, with these nodes, you will be asked to lose your dependency on another person at certain times in life.

The trouble with being so dependent on another for our comfort is that we can become overly concerned we will lose them and, in order not to, bend over backwards for them. Eventually, our own personality may get lost. At the extreme end of the scale, if you are really desperate to hold on to a partner, you can end up becoming a doormat or a victim of abuse; you become so desperate not to be alone that you will tolerate almost anything.

If this is the case, there will certainly come a point when you will leave. How long this will take depends on you. If your birth chart has several planets that are fixed, you will be reluctant to make changes, so it may take you longer than someone who has mutable or cardinal planets. Some people leave at the first sign of trouble, some wait and try to compromise, and some stay long after they should have left out of a sense of guilt, responsibility, or fear. Sadly, there are people out there who are incredibly clever at manipulating others, and if your desire for a partnership is overriding, you may be a willing (if naïve) participant. Certainly, at some point you will find yourself on your own, looking into the mirror and wondering who you actually are. Can you stand on your own two feet?

The answer, of course, is yes. But to do so requires you to evaluate your innate talents and abilities to find out who you really are when another isn't there to take your attention away from your inner search. Instead of thinking of another, you will be able to put yourself first. In effect, you will go from being compromising to being self-centred, but this is a necessary task in this life. You are to learn all about yourself and how to manage alone. Go to restaurants and cafés on your own, visit the theatre, and even travel abroad. It will be a learning curve, but you will discover how to express your own needs without having to take another's into account. This might feel scary at first, but in time, you may even come to enjoy being a single person, although your comfort zone will always be a relationship.

SOUTH NODE EIGHTH HOUSE ➡ NORTH NODE SECOND HOUSE

Comfort Zones: *Accepting other's values and possessions; relying on others*

Challenges: *Standing on your own two feet; finding self-worth by developing a talent or ability*

POSSESSION AXIS

These areas of life are on the possession axis and are related to the things you work for yourself and the things you get from other people. The eighth house is what *other* people own. It can literally refer to material possessions, wealth, and property, but it also encompasses other's values and beliefs. Traditionally, this house is the area of inheritance and death, and seen in this light, it is obvious why. It is usually through death that we obtain inheritances. So, the eighth house is what we get from others, either by death or by choosing to live by another's rules. The opposite house, the second, is all about what we get through our own efforts and our own hard work.

YOUR LAST LIFE: YOUR SOUTH NODE

If your south node is in the eighth house, you spent your last lifetime abiding by someone else's rules in order to maintain your security. This could be as simple as being supported by another: a marriage partner, a parent, a boss, or even a sibling. Perhaps you were unable, for whatever reason, to provide for yourself. In order to have financial protection, you would have had to live by another's rules and wishes. This is an unspoken but very real aspect of the eighth house: the one who pays calls the shots.

Another aspect of the eighth house is psychology. This is because there is a certain amount of psychological manipulation that occurs between two people who are in this dynamic. The eighth house is traditionally ruled by Scorpio, which can—and will—manipulate in order to control. So, it may seem simple to be looked after by others, but Scorpio is a deeply compelling sign. Sex, control, jealousy, and manipulation are some of its areas. In the old days (and sometimes still) women were subjected in marriage. They lost all of their property and money, which was given to the husband on their wedding day. In some countries, this still happens, or women are forced to live a certain way if they want to be looked after by another. Wherever there is any form of control in return for something, we are in eighth-house territory.

An extreme problem with this house occurs when someone cannot achieve any worldly status themselves and so decides not to wait to inherit wealth, but chooses to take it: to steal or even kill in order to get their hands on the goods. Or it may be that the control someone is under is so extreme, in either a sexual or possessive way, that they kill the perpetrator. Thus, this eighth house is an area of varied and numerous levels of control, from the very lowest expression (committing murder to gain material wealth) to the more accepted (one person looking after another who is unable to care for themselves). When one cares for another with entirely altruistic motives, they embody the highest spiritual energy of Scorpio.

THIS LIFETIME: YOUR NORTH NODE

Whatever happened to you in the last life, you carry into this life the expectation that you will be cared for by others. In order for this to happen, you allow them to call the shots. It feels natural for you to adapt to another to gain protection and security. You feel a deep sense of rightness being looked after by another, regardless of social norms. However, because of this dependence on another, you failed to develop your own talents in your last life.

Now, you are unable to stand on your own two feet in the world, and even holding down a steady job will feel difficult. Certainly, providing for yourself in a material sense is now viewed askance, if not mildly horrific—you simply don't know how to go about it. Your natural inclination will be to cleave to another as soon as you are able. In return, you will try to be all that they ask.

But your learning curve in this life is to try and stand alone. Therefore, life will present various opportunities for you to develop this ability. It is unlikely the rug will be pulled out from under you completely, but in one way or another, a time will come when you will have to confront the second house and try to provide for yourself. It won't be easy for you to break this reliance on other people; you feel safe having others in charge. But bit by bit, try to work on developing a talent of yours so that you have skills to offer. This will create a sense of self-worth, and you might just find that you like feeling this way, of being a cog in the wheel of commerce, of knowing you are capable of standing alone in a material sense, of being free to have your own values and beliefs without fear of losing your home or your support.

The bottom line is that the second house is all about your own sense of self-worth. There is a feeling of value, an innate self-assuredness when you can provide for yourself and others, a sense of confidence in managing finances and building security via your possessions. Being able to do all of this yourself has a strong impact on your self-esteem. Sweep everything else away and the bald fact remains that when someone looks after us, we lose our place in the world, not only in our own eyes, but in others'. We are perceived as a reflection of someone else: someone's wife, someone's mother, someone's husband, someone's father, someone's employee, and so forth. By developing even one of your own talents and bringing it forth into the world, you will build your confidence in yourself as a human being who has something that others want. Your life challenge is relying on yourself to provide security.

SOUTH NODE NINTH HOUSE ➡ NORTH NODE THIRD HOUSE

Comfort Zones: Being philosophical/thinking for yourself; living in isolation; private research; teaching at a higher level

Challenges: Interacting with the collective; living amongst others; teaching what you know

---

THINKING AXIS

The ninth and third houses are on the thinking axis. That's because they deal with thoughts and communication. So, from a young age, you will experience challenges in life that centre around these issues. The ninth house is all about individual thoughts and ideas, and the third is about the collective identity and what we are all taught to believe.

YOUR LAST LIFE: YOUR SOUTH NODE

The ninth house is high in the chart, and when there is an emphasis high in the chart, we see life from a wider, more intuitive perspective. There is a distinct but subtle feeling of objectively looking down at the activity in the collective, at the bottom of the chart, while being slightly removed from it. This is how you feel, because your last life would have been spent in this ninth-house area. This is not a totally isolated house, but your life would have provided opportunities for private research and space in which to develop your own philosophies and beliefs.

While in this life, you may listen to people in authority, it is likely that you don't believe everything you are told. It is not that you automatically dismiss other people's ideas, but rather that you naturally sift through them. Even if an idea appears feasible, you must put it to the test: Does the idea work? Is it valid? In other words, you make up your own mind. You think for yourself and only accept what intuitively feels right. This is what the ninth house is all about.

You are wise enough to know that many of the things we are taught are perfectly valid. Therefore, you can see there is no need to discard every idea and thought, only those that are outdated. In the last life, you developed this freedom of thought. You didn't want to be tied intellectually to any point of view or a group with fixed beliefs. You wanted to explore the world in your search for the eternal truth, the meaning to everything. *Who are we?* you would have asked. *Why are we here? What is our purpose?*

To answer these questions and many more besides, you would have spent your last life reading, analysing, listening, travelling, and studying. You might have been an archaeologist, an explorer, a journalist or travel writer, a university lecturer, or just lucky enough to have the money to spend your life studying due to your pure love of research. Spending time thinking, studying, and researching often meant being alone, whether in a study, an office, a library, or even in the countryside to find the peace necessary to form ideas. Because you spent so much time alone in the last life, you still have the desire to remove yourself from the busy world and live in some form of quiet isolation.

THIS LIFETIME: YOUR NORTH NODE

All the private study of your last life means you bring with you into this life a wisdom beyond your years. From an early age, you would have listened to others but made up your own mind. Scams have never misled you—you see the falsity in people's words and ideas. You're naturally clever and wise. There is a surety in your beliefs that is appealing to others, who look to you to advise and/or teach them.

The third house is at the bottom of the chart in the collective. The collective is the local environment. This means family, siblings, friends, teachers, and anyone and everyone we meet in the course of daily life. As we grow, these people teach us what we are supposed to think, which is the way *they* think. We believe what we are taught. It must be correct, surely, because our parents said so, and our teachers said so, and our religious leaders said so. The collective's shared beliefs and ideas provide a form of security; everyone thinks the same and teaches the same, and no one questions the validity.

In this life, your north nodes are in the third house, so this is the area you are being asked to move towards. You are being asked to go down into the busy collective, to mix with everyone and teach what you know. You will baulk at this. Having spent a lifetime in quiet contemplation, the idea of heading into the noisy world is a bit daunting. You will resist. The collective doesn't think as you do; they live in a busy, noisy, chaotic world—or so it seems to you, in comparison to your life of quiet contemplation.

But as your life progresses, circumstances will conspire that offer you opportunities to join the collective one way or another. Having spent a lifetime developing your personal philosophy, you are now being asked to pass on what you know, but in a way everyone can understand. This could be done via teaching, writing, or speaking; the third house is all about communication, so many methods can be used. In today's world, we have podcasts, YouTube, Zoom, and Skype that run alongside the more traditional ways of teaching and learning. It won't be long before these are superseded by even quicker and more effective ways of communicating. But it doesn't matter how your knowledge reaches the third house so long as it does. Choose what suits you.

The main difficulty ninth-house people face is explaining their philosophies and ideas in a way everyone can understand. There is no good in expressing a profound theory if it is incomprehensible to those who are listening. This is another challenge inherent with these nodes: you will have to learn how to present your wisdom in an accessible way.

When the south node is in the ninth house, there is always the desire to return to your ivory tower, to live quietly, and to follow your own inclinations. But life is asking you to pass on all you know via the third house, and finding an accessible way of doing so that balances the north and south nodes is your learning curve.

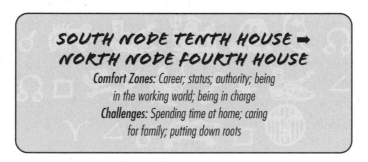

SOUTH NODE TENTH HOUSE ➡ NORTH NODE FOURTH HOUSE

Comfort Zones: Career; status; authority; being in the working world; being in charge
Challenges: Spending time at home; caring for family; putting down roots

INDIVIDUAL AXIS

This axis is all about our deepest roots versus our highest position in the world. In other words, where we come from, our home and birth family (the fourth house), and what we strive to be recognized for in the world, via our career (the tenth house).

YOUR LAST LIFE: YOUR SOUTH NODE

With the south node in the tenth house, from an early age you would have felt you were an individual, and that you were far more talented than those around you. You inherently knew who you are and what you are capable of. Therefore, you've always wanted to stand out from the rest of the collective, including your early environment and the people you grew up with. You feel you have something special to offer, and you have an intuitive knowledge of the best way to go about it. Because of this, it is likely you would have left your family while young to forge your way in the world.

The tenth house is the highest part of a birth chart. It shows the best you can be as an individual. In this life, you don't want to be lumped in with your contemporaries. You want to succeed in the world, often via a career of some sort. The reason you feel this way, and the reason you have such an innate talent in your career of choice, is because this is what you did in the last life. You found a job you loved and you worked hard at it, and you eventually found success. You became a leader in your field; you probably had your own business. These skills followed you into this life.

THIS LIFETIME: YOUR NORTH NODE

There is no doubt you *will* succeed in your chosen career because this is what you did in the last life, so it is second nature to you. You naturally understand how to go about your work, the best methods to use, the right people to approach, and how to market your talents and/or expand your business. It's intuitive. You are an entrepreneur, even if you work for someone else. You naturally take charge, and others have complete trust in your abilities.

Because of this inner certainty, you may have decided a formal education was unnecessary. Many entrepreneurs left school at a young age. Formal education isn't for everyone, and it certainly isn't for you. Although you felt traditional learning was dull and not going to teach you much, you are very intelligent. It is likely you will catch up on this learning as you go through life anyway by reading widely, delving into many subjects, and having an open mind.

Traditional learning isn't necessary for you because your knowledge from a past life means you don't really need paper qualifications to impress a boss. If you need to know any rules or regulations, your cleverness makes it easy to find the necessary information. So, this is your comfort zone: your career. You feel right at home being the boss, being in charge, or certainly being in a respected position within your workplace. Although you don't necessarily seek admiration from others, you do get it because of your focused mindset and good work ethic.

In this life, your north nodes are in the fourth house, which oversees home and family. As much as you love your family, the idea of staying at home all day is, quite frankly, scary. What would you do with yourself? How could you manage without that admiration and respect you are so accustomed to? Without that daily interplay between you and others?

In the last life, you spent very little time at home. Lots of things may have caused this. Apart from your high-profile career, perhaps you travelled a lot for work, socialized after working hours, or had someone at home who took care of the more mundane aspects of life so you didn't have to—or maybe you were a workaholic. Most likely, it was a combination of these.

The fourth house is a caring, supportive, empathic place where care and attention is focused on family first and foremost. There is a very emotional aspect to the fourth house. Though you have experience building your life by focusing on worldly matters and personal accomplishment and find it hard to relate to the nurturing side of the fourth, this is what you are being asked to do in this life.

Your task now is to focus more on your home and family. This does not mean you have to walk away from work and become a person who looks after others in the home, but you are being asked to try to embody the energy of the fourth. Maybe one aspect of being in the home appeals?

It will be best if you voluntarily choose to spend time in the fourth house area of life. Often, people with these nodes take up something they've always been interested in, like gardening, cooking, or a hobby that can be done from home. But it will be hard to be in a position where you aren't recognized out in the world, and you will naturally try to be in charge and in control of the home because that is what you are accustomed to. This can cause relationship issues. Think about it: if a partner or family member has always been in control of the household and you suddenly take charge, they might feel aggrieved and usurped, especially if your methods are different. You'll want to run the household like you ran your business and take charge of any situation, but nurturing has a different feel and method altogether. This will be a big learning curve, which you may or may not manage.

This is the one south/north node position that, at some point in life, you will be forced to confront because there usually comes a time in everyone's life when a career, or being out and about every day, is impossible. Some with these nodes take on voluntary work to fill their days after retirement. Some continue to head out to work, even if part-time, well into their eighties and beyond; they are proud to contribute and love the admiration they get when people are amazed they still work "at their age." These are some of the tactics people use to avoid confronting the fourth house. But, at some point, most of us will be forced to stay home, maybe due to failing health or ability. If you stubbornly refuse every suggestion of the universe, it often pulls the rug out from under us so we have no alternative. When this happens, some people retire and actively build a new life around the home. And it is at this point you might discover that, actually, being home isn't so bad after all.

There is no doubt that our north node area of life is never our true comfort zone, but most of us find a certain aspect of it appealing, and this is all the universe expects. As you learn to balance your nodes, you can continue to head out to work, where you feel right at home.

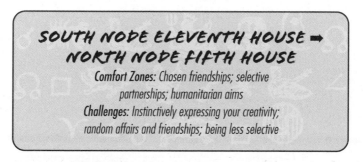

SOUTH NODE ELEVENTH HOUSE → NORTH NODE FIFTH HOUSE

Comfort Zones: Chosen friendships; selective partnerships; humanitarian aims

Challenges: Instinctively expressing your creativity; random affairs and friendships; being less selective

FRIENDSHIP AXIS

These two houses have to do with our interactions with others, which is why they are on what is called the friendship axis. The eleventh house is about selective friendships, whereas the fifth deals with random encounters where we make no judgments but accept people as they are.

YOUR LAST LIFE: YOUR SOUTH NODE

The eleventh house is all about sharing our time with those we have a lot in common with, those with high ideals just like our own and, possibly, humanitarian aims.

With your south nodes in this house, you consciously chose the people you mixed with in the last life. You saw yourself as an individual with certain ideals, and you only wanted to rub shoulders with people who shared those same ideals. It might have been as simple as something like joining a birdwatching group because that was your passion, or a hiking group because you enjoyed adventurous walking. On the more extreme end, you may have only formed links with organizations that had humanitarian aims.

You felt really comfortable and at home with people who had the same values as you. You had an inner drive to be part of some cultural, artistic, or idealistic venture. It was this sense of togetherness and belonging that bolstered your self-worth and gave you your place in the world. You sought out like-minded friends, and you were extremely discerning in your choice of relationships and friendships—you wouldn't have wasted the time of day on people you thought you had nothing in common with. There might have been a sense of looking down on others. This is because the eleventh house is at the top of the chart, which meant you had an objective, refined palate when it came to other people, and you couldn't help making judgements.

Because there was a conscious detachment from the hubbub of life, you rarely acted on impulse or instinct and never allowed your emotions to override your logic, which was always on the horizon. In this humanitarian house, you felt you had better fish to fry in life than getting drawn into human passions and dramas; in fact, you preferred it when human emotions were not part of the picture at all. Your personal relationships would have been few—your judgemental approach applied to this area of your life too.

THIS LIFETIME: YOUR NORTH NODE

With the south node in the eleventh house you might, even now, instantly dismiss some people as being beneath you. You come into this lifetime still carrying the need to be careful of who you choose as friends. This selectivity can have its downsides—there is a fine line between being discerning and being snobbish. It will be equally easy to end up being a bit fanatical about your ideals, either forming or joining groups that hope to change the world. This can be good or bad, depending on the group and its methods for instigating change. The other pitfall is that if the group disappoints you in some way, or if more than one group fails, you may be tempted to withdraw from everyone and live mostly alone, as a semi-recluse. Then, you'd feel out of synch with everyone and believe that no one really understands you at all, and the more you think like this, the more you retreat into yourself.

But let's assume the best outcome. If you have the south nodes in this house, you will measure your self-worth not on what you own but on the friendships you have. It makes you feel good to know you mix with the movers and shakers of the day: politicians, lawyers, royalty, people who are someone in the world. And, having reached this inner circle, the last thing you want to do is hobnob with anyone you consider inferior. How can they possibly understand your view and perspective? What on earth will you say to them?

This selectivity will start young; you might only have one or two chosen friends in school. Throughout the first half of your life, your friendship circle will be small but consciously chosen. A lot of thought will go into who you keep as a friend and what you want from them. Every time life gets hard, you will go to your chosen group, and that sense of belonging makes you feel secure and happy. You might even go so far as to prefer to spend time with them over your own family. As you age, this will apply to relationships too. You won't have many, and your prospective partner will have to jump through hoops to reach the inner you.

In this life, you are being asked to consider dipping your toe into the opposite house, the fifth. This area of life has no appeal for you whatsoever. The fifth house deals with self-expression, so it covers all forms of creativity, from acting to artistic and literary endeavours. Even having children is a fifth-house activity—they are an act of creation, after all.

The fifth house is down at the bottom of the chart, in the collective area, so you'll be asked to accept the people you meet regardless of who they are or where they come from. The fifth house is sort of like a bar, where it's possible to make casual friendships of all sorts, both romantic and platonic. That is exactly what you are being asked to do in this life. A lot of people will pass through your life because meeting them in this way means they rarely stay around for long, and that is okay. This is the house of enjoyment, of having fun, of letting your hair down. It is the place where brief romantic liaisons happen. The whole fifth house is imbued with that sense of abandon and playfulness that children have: they live in the moment, easily make friends, and rarely, if ever, judge.

Just reading this will fill you with a mild horror. No way do you want to mix with just anyone! Luckily, life is not asking you to completely change your mindset, but to give one aspect a try. You also have your whole life to integrate fifth-house energy, so there is no need to leap immediately into a different way of behaving. Life will offer opportunities to embody the fifth as time goes on. These opportunities will come at the perfect time, so there is no need for you to do anything at all except be open to the possibilities when they appear.

One way to move towards this north node is by developing your inner creativity. Have you considered becoming an amateur actor, perhaps? Actors rarely go amongst the audience but are held in awe by them, which might sit better with you. It could also involve being part of a specialized group, which might also resonate. Or, do you like to write? Why not write about the subject that you feel most interested in, be it birdwatching or hiking or your idealistic aims? This would bring you into contact with people you might not normally mix with. Photography is another way of showing the beauty or the suffering in the world; they say a picture speaks a thousand words. Art is a very expressive way of explaining your beliefs. Love affairs, too, bring one down to the most basic of actions and emotions, so perhaps you will fall in love with someone that in the past you would have considered "unsuitable."

There are many ways in which you can reach the fifth house of self-expression without losing your sense of self-worth or your selective friendship group while still opening up a whole new world. Know that you will always have that special group of friends behind you as you experiment with the untried and untested. Life isn't asking you to toss everything that works for you; it is just asking you to give the fifth house a try.

When anyone is being asked to come down from the top of the chart to the bottom of the chart in their lifetime, there is a need to communicate in a way that an ordinary person can relate to and understand. It will be necessary to shift your perspective by taking the needs of the collective into account. No matter how good a writer, actor, or speaker you might be, it will fall on stony ground unless you express it in a way that those in the collective can understand.

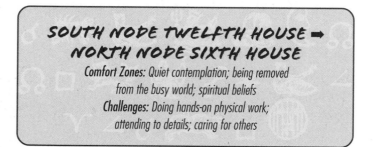

SOUTH NODE TWELFTH HOUSE ➡ NORTH NODE SIXTH HOUSE

Comfort Zones: Quiet contemplation; being removed from the busy world; spiritual beliefs
Challenges: Doing hands-on physical work; attending to details; caring for others

BEING AXIS

These houses are on the being axis. The twelfth house is all about our own spiritual search for the meaning of life. To do this requires a lot of time alone to meditate, contemplate, and assess our own beliefs. The opposite house, the sixth, is all about survival—making ourselves useful and showcasing our talents and abilities in a practical way, literally rolling up our sleeves and getting on with real service and hands-on work.

YOUR LAST LIFE: YOUR SOUTH NODE

In the last life, you inhabited the twelfth house, so your life would have been spent in quiet, reflective thought. Because your south node is here, you come into this life with the calm serenity of being centred in your spirit. You spent a lot of time developing your spiritual beliefs and ideas in the past life. There are many ways this could have been achieved. You may have served a religion or worked in the service of mankind in some selfless way. Sometimes even those with busy lives find the time and space to meditate, so regardless of what you actually did, you would have spent a lot of time analysing your life and developing your spiritual beliefs. Think of someone like Mother Teresa, who worked very hard selflessly serving others throughout her long life. So, it is not so much what you did but the way you did it. You may have started out just like everyone else, but all the time you were developing your higher spiritual self.

Because the twelfth house is the spiritual house and is far removed from the striving, noisy, busy world, while it's likely that you did have a reclusive lifestyle, there are areas where hard work in the service of mankind can be done. Hospitals of all sorts come under this house, as does any institution that is removed from the world where rest, recuperation, and time for spiritual contemplation are possible. That's why religious houses are here, as are prisons. One hopes those who commit crimes against humanity will, given time for thought, reflect on their deeds and adjust their behaviours and ideas. It is entirely possible you lived or worked in a hospital, in a prison, or in a facility removed from the world in the last life. You may have been a nun, a monk, or a devout follower of a particular religion. Or, at the other end of the scale, you may have been imprisoned in some way yourself, giving you the time and space to contemplate life. No matter which path you took, you came into this life with this same requirement for isolation, for space to think and just "be." This is your comfort area, so to face the world in practical terms will not be easy for you.

THIS LIFETIME: YOUR NORTH NODE

The difficulty with this south node is that life is demanding. You have developed the tools for rest, peace, and contemplation, but when faced with the (as you see it) noisy, busy, chaotic world, you shrink back. All that jostling for position, striving to be the best, the stressful working world with its never-ending demands, trying to be all things to all people while putting food on the table and keeping a roof over your head—it's overwhelmingly scary. Not because you don't want to be of use, but because you have no idea how to go about it. If you did indeed spend your last life in some form of retreat, chosen or otherwise, it will be really hard to get to grips with your new role, because you aren't worldly wise. Yet, as life progresses, events will occur that mean you have to venture out into the world like everyone else. You will have to develop the ability to earn money. The sixth house is literally the house of service or, to put it another way, the work house, so you'll be required to roll up your sleeves and do real physical labour. In the last life, your mind would have been focused on higher matters, and it is doubtful you noticed who cooked the food, mopped the floor, or organized the finances. This time, you will be encouraged to lower your eyes and notice these details, and when you see a job that needs doing, to do it.

With these nodal placements, there is an innate understanding that if a sacrifice needs to be made, you must willingly bend your shoulder to the wheel. It's likely you are kind, compassionate, and non-judgemental, accepting of people from all walks of life. In reality, you can rarely say no to people, especially those who are stronger and more forceful—which is just about everyone when you are from the twelfth house. You will find, without any conscious effort on your part, that life will manoeuvre you into a position where you are required to go against your natural inclinations and become involved in the hubbub of life. You are usually given strong planetary positions to help you, like having the sun down in the collective as well.

While you question who you really are and what your purpose is (because that's how you spent the last life), you will be asked to face the demands of life in their rawest form. You might question if you have any abilities that are useful in the world and how you can contribute. You won't know what is expected of you or quite how to go about it. In fact, if you do succeed at mastering something you can offer the world, it will instil in you a greater sense of self-confidence.

With these nodes, you can always refresh and restore yourself with quiet contemplation and stillness, but you have no problem with the sacrifices demanded. When you find a skill or talent that is valuable to society, you will do whatever you can to help others. Thus, in reality, these nodes are the easiest to balance because of your self-sacrificing nature and the innate humility you learnt in the last life.

three
The Nodes and the Signs

The house positions of the south and north node show where your life will be guided, whereas the astrological sign they occupy will show you *how* this can be achieved. Remember that the north node will show up on a birth chart, but most sites do not show the south node. Here is a list to help you determine your south node sign.

- If your north node is in Aries, your south node will be in Libra.
- If your north node is in Taurus, your south node will be in Scorpio.
- If your north node is in Gemini, your south node will be in Sagittarius.

- If your north node is in Cancer, your south node will be in Capricorn.
- If your north node is in Leo, your south node will be in Aquarius.
- If your north node is in Virgo, your south node will be in Pisces.
- If your north node is in Libra, your south node will be in Aries.
- If your north node is in Scorpio, your south node will be in Taurus.
- If your north node is in Sagittarius, your south node will be in Gemini.
- If your north node is in Capricorn, your south node will be in Cancer.
- If your north node is in Aquarius, your south node will be in Leo.
- If your north node is in Pisces, your south node will be in Virgo.

Once you've read the section that applies to your nodal placements, take some time to analyse how these signs are at work in your life. Your south node sign characteristics should feel natural and comfortable, whereas your north node sign traits should feel unfamiliar or like a work in progress. Life will guide you towards your north node sign via small steps.

> ### SOUTH NODE ARIES →
> ### NORTH NODE LIBRA
> **Aries Traits:** *Fast; impatient; talkative; proactive;*
> *loves a challenge; independent; confrontational*
> **Libra Traits:** *Compromising; peace-loving; harmony-seeking*

YOUR LAST LIFE: ARIES SOUTH NODE

In this life, you are moving from the traits of Aries to the traits of Libra. If you read the traits of both Aries and Libra, you'll be thinking that in no way whatsoever are you interested in keeping everyone happy! This is because in the last life you spent most of your time becoming familiar with the sign of Aries.

You learned how to be independent and confident; you developed your individuality, discovered your personal strengths and weaknesses (which you would have tried to overcome), and came to rely on only yourself. You learned how to forge new pathways, to initiate actions, and to take charge. Therefore, you come into this life with an inner confidence in your own abilities as well as the desire to be dependent on no one but yourself. You now prefer to be the boss, and to press on with the business of life without taking others into account. This means you really dislike asking anyone for advice, or even for their opinion. You are perfectly capable of having the buck stop with you. You are a "live by the sword, die by the sword" person.

Your problem area in the last life would have been how this independent stance affected your relationships. It is hard to be an independent, capable person if you have to take the feelings and opinions of others into account, so it is likely you ended up living alone. This might have been through personal choice or because partners grew tired of not having their words heard and appreciated. Or perhaps you did have a partner, and they accepted that you had your own life and made the best of it.

The sign of Aries does not compromise. It is the sign of "me, myself, and I." This is as it should be, so there is no blame attached. To be of use to the world around you, you first need to know who you are and what you have to offer, so this position of the south node in Aries deliberately allowed you to discover things about yourself as well as how to express the qualities of Aries.

THIS LIFETIME: LIBRA NORTH NODE

Your north node sign is in Libra. This sign is ruled by Venus, which is the planet of love and harmony. Yes, it is the exact opposite of Aries. Libra is all about creating and maintaining a harmonious long-term relationship, one based on compromise and consideration for each other. Libra's symbol is the scales, which shows their desire to balance all arguments and opinions—Libra finds a middle ground that keeps everyone happy, or at least appeased. Libra is an air sign, so it listens to what people have to say and then endeavours to be fair to all parties.

It's pretty clear this will not appeal to you in the least. You don't need to be dependent on anyone else. You don't even like discussing things with other people—you just go out and do what you want. You never bother to ask for anyone's opinion about what you intend to do, nor do you listen to feedback and then think about what you've heard. Your focus is on yourself; you trust your own judgement because that's what you are so familiar with. It is alien to you to act in a way that keeps everyone else happy. This, then, is your challenge in this life.

No one wants to confront their north node house or sign, but throughout your life, opportunities will present themselves to you that allow you to learn how to do this. It is likely you will avoid a commitment for as long as you can (you may feel it threatens your identity), but no person is an island. Perhaps one day you will meet someone special. To keep them in your life, compromise will be necessary. There are many ways life can gradually encourage you to think of others, and you'll learn to balance your inner confidence in yourself with your need for a committed and supportive partnership.

How you go about this, and how these new lessons will present themselves, depends on which houses your nodes are in. The south node house will be where you act independently and the north node house is the area in which you must learn to compromise with others.

Remember that there is no hurry, nor do you have to take any conscious action towards your north node until life presents you with the opportunity to do so. Take small steps, and be open to the signals for change.

SOUTH NODE TAURUS → NORTH NODE SCORPIO

Taurus Traits: Stubborn; patient; resistant to change; earthy and tactile; security minded; practical; unemotional; possessive
Scorpio Traits: Highly emotional; dramatic; passionate; driven; possessive; manipulative

YOUR LAST LIFE: TAURUS SOUTH NODE

While reading the Taurus descriptions, you'll be thinking, *Yep, that's me.* But when you scan the Scorpio traits, you will probably feel no connection to them at all. Emotional? Dramatic? No way! But you will be, by the end of your life. Maybe not as emotional as a true Scorpio, but throughout life, your emotional side will blossom. These shifts and changes come slowly, so all you have to do is to allow life's experiences to show you the way.

Right now, you inhabit the traits of Taurus because this was your comfort area in a previous life. Like the symbol for Taurus, the bull, you came into this life with fixed ideas, incredible strength, and steely determination. So fixed were your ideas that you are immovable; you resist change. Therefore, this sign more than any other may have trouble adapting to new circumstances in this lifetime.

You would have worked hard and accumulated material wealth, or at the very least, security. Taurus is the sign that stands on its own two feet. As it rules the second house of security and finance, this was your focus. It's likely you still feel the need to build financial security and create a safe wall around yourself from the winds of change. Both mentally and materially, you like to do things the way that feel comfortable, and you resist any sort of alteration. Once you are stable and comfortable, nothing will move you. This desire to hang on to things will make you quite possessive of romantic partners; you may see partners in the same way as you see your house and belongings—as your property.

Introspection is not something you do. Work is your forte. Analysing and questioning things is of no interest to you. Your aim is to make sure you surround yourself with security, and once you've done that, you make everything as comfortable as possible and stay put. Taurus is a tactile sign and enjoys hard-earned rewards with gusto: eating, drinking, and any sensual pleasures. For example, you love cuddling up to a loved one to watch television after a great meal. Esoteric ideas are of no interest because they provide nothing of practical use.

THIS LIFETIME: SCORPIO NORTH NODE

In this life, you are being asked to move gradually towards the sign of Scorpio. It's likely you raised your eyebrows in disbelief when you read about Scorpio, but this is the type of person you will become as life progresses. Scorpio will open the door to a more emotive version of you. Scorpio is full of passions (and yes, that includes the physical delights), but it is also an emotional sign, and Taurus is not. So, you will move towards becoming a more emotional person throughout your life. When you feel this happening, go along with it if you can. Allow emotions some space.

Scorpio rules the eighth house, which indicates being looked after by others, amongst other things. The security you need so deeply—the security you take pride in being able to provide for yourself—may be threatened. Instead of providing for yourself and others, you may find yourself in a position of having to take from others. Being dependent on someone else will be your hardest lesson. Basically, your previous life was one of giving security to others, but now you have to learn to receive.

The way you think, too, will alter. Circumstances and experiences will force you to become more introspective. This will gradually lead to a letting go of material things and an acceptance of spirituality. You will start questioning things and looking beneath the surface to find the underlying purpose of life.

Both these signs are fixed, and both are possessive to a certain degree. The difference in signs that you will be welcoming in your lifetime is a deeper sensitivity to the unseen forces of life, an acceptance that just because you can't see it doesn't mean it isn't there.

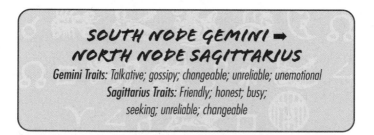

SOUTH NODE GEMINI ➡ NORTH NODE SAGITTARIUS

Gemini Traits: Talkative; gossipy; changeable; unreliable; unemotional
Sagittarius Traits: Friendly; honest; busy; seeking; unreliable; changeable

YOUR LAST LIFE: GEMINI SOUTH NODE

At first glance, it may look like there is not much difference between Gemini and Sagittarius; they seem fairly similar. And they are, to a certain extent. Both are busy and friendly, which therefore makes them unreliable. Neither like deadlines or formal structure to their day; both love words and listening to people. But their motivations—and, therefore, what they glean from their conversations—is entirely different.

Let's start with Gemini, because this is the sign you are comfortable with. This sign rules communication. It is the Geminis of the world who are such good teachers, educators, messengers, and gossips. This is an air sign, so you'll flit through life like a butterfly, landing here and there for a moment, picking up bits of information, and delivering them at the next stop—or at a future date. Our world is very media-led right now, which you adore. If we did a survey of people in the media, from journalists to movie stars and talk-show hosts to comedians and anchors of political programs—the whole gamut—it's reasonable to assume there would be a high percentage of Geminis in these fields. Most are fascinated by technology and the written and spoken word, so where there is communication and language, Geminis abound.

Witty comedians, clever interviewers, gossipy talk-show hosts, YouTubers and influencers, media movers and shakers of the day—all are the personification of the sign of Gemini. Like them, you will love to be at the centre of what's happening and mixing with people of like mind. What's the point of outdated information? To be in the know, you have to be at the forefront of things.

With a Gemini south node, this is the environment that suits you best. Even if you haven't reached dizzying heights in your career, you'll be the one in the office (or in your family) that brings cheer by joking around and lightening the mood. You dislike heavy stuff. That goes for relationships too; if a person keeps it light and friendly, you'll keep coming back. If partners get possessive, jealous, and emotional, you'll flee the scene.

THIS LIFETIME: SAGITTARIUS NORTH NODE

As life progresses, your mindset will alter. It will happen slowly, in a barely perceptible way, but by the time retirement beckons, you will think more like a Sagittarius.

What's the difference? Well, Sagittarius is a fire sign, so it has energy and warmth. The energy that drives you will still be a natural curiosity, but instead of flitting away immediately, subjects will start to intrigue you more; you'll want to dig deeper, to get to the truth. For Geminis, the truth is irrelevant—it's the information you're after, and you don't want to do anything with it but pass it on. But Sagittarius wants to know *why*. Somewhere along the way, you will start to question what you are being told. Is it the truth?

Our world is full of information. As a Gemini, that is enough. But as a Sagittarius, you no longer believe what people say just because they say it. You will question things. Subjects will be studied in more depth. You'll discover a whole new esoteric side to life, a wider vision than when you were like Gemini. You might question the existence of a god or wonder where we came from, or perhaps you'll discover a dusty tomb somewhere that intrigues you enough to uncover what it has to say, to deeply explore our world and its mysteries.

Sagittarius still teaches, but it does so with a reasoned wisdom. It doesn't teach what we learn every day; it teaches people higher thoughts and deeper subjects. It encourages listeners to think for themselves and find their own answers. Rather than passing on surface-level facts in the Gemini way, it passes on wisdom. Communication is still key, but it's the content that will change.

On a more prosaic level, where once you were happy to live closely with everyone and accept all the customs that come along with society, the more you move into Sagittarius, the more you will question these traditional beliefs and customs. Your mindset will go through shifts and changes, and you may find your own way of practicing a faith, or you'll discard it altogether.

Although you will still meet many people, instead of just chatting and joking, you will want to pick their brains about their ideas, and then you'll seek solitude to think about their ideas and analyse if they have meaning for you. Once you become more Sagittarian, you'll be less inclined to mix with all and sundry because you will want your conversations to be with people of like mind who can discuss ideas in an intellectual way. To do this might mean you decline invitations to parties and events that you once would have loved.

Relationships are still an issue. The signs Gemini and Sagittarius, while different elements (one being air, one fire), are both of the mind, not the body. While you may have partnerships, it's more likely you'll prefer to stay single so you can roam free, both physically and mentally. For this reason, both Gemini and Sagittarius prove unreliable partners. However, it is your thought processes that are your lessons in this lifetime—relationships are not the issue.

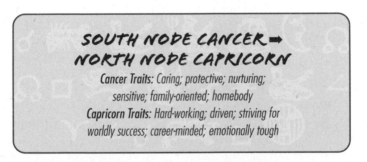

SOUTH NODE CANCER ➡ NORTH NODE CAPRICORN

Cancer Traits: Caring; protective; nurturing; sensitive; family-oriented; homebody
Capricorn Traits: Hard-working; driven; striving for worldly success; career-minded; emotionally tough

YOUR LAST LIFE: CANCER SOUTH NODE

The sign of Cancer is your comfort zone. You come into this life with a kind and caring nature, a willingness to look after others, and a drive to protect those you love from harm. You possess an inner compass that detects when your loved ones are unhappy or hurting, and you have the ability to heal those wounds with your nurturing.

You make people feel special and adored. They know you will always be there for them, and that whatever age or stage in life, you will be their safety net—at least in emotional terms. You have an open-door policy for those you love and wrap them in care and nurturing as soon as they step over the threshold.

Cancer is a strong sign. Yes, you are emotional and caring, but you are also proactive and capable of huge personal sacrifices to serve those you love; you always put yourself last. "Those you love" does not just apply to your own family. Anyone and everyone who finds themselves in your orbit is "adopted" as family, and you try to be there for them in any way you can. Your loving, caring nature extends to your career as well, so you often choose a field that allows you to express this.

This is who you are at the start of your life, because this is what you became used to in the last life. It is now an innate and natural way for you to act, so you do it without conscious thought. It feels like a natural extension of you as an individual.

THIS LIFETIME: CAPRICORN NORTH NODE

Consider Capricorn traits. There are a couple that will come naturally, like working hard; you don't have a problem with that. But you are not career-minded, generally. Most Cancerians focus on the home and loved ones, not on their career per se, so worldly success is not something you strive for.

Gradually, though, as life progresses, in small shifts and changes, you will find yourself becoming more like a Capricorn. You won't love your family any less, instead finding that they don't need you to look after them as you once did. They may become very independent, or they may resist asking you to help for whatever reason, or they may move too far away for you to be able to care for them, or perhaps with age comes the inability to look after others as you once did—there are any number of ways your loved ones can become independent of you.

Your lesson in this life will be a long time coming. Capricorn is a sign blessed with longevity. It is ruled by Saturn, which is a hard taskmaster. Saturn creates obstacles and blocks, and it takes you back to square one time and again until you get it right. If you are veering off course, not heading in the correct direction, Saturn will slam the door in your face until you find the one door that will open. Then, and only then, will the obstacles fall away. With age will come wisdom. This long road to knowledge has taught you a lot, so you have much to impart to the world.

The challenge with these nodes is to accept that you are not needed as you once were, that your hands-on caring days are over. Instead, you are being given the time and space to develop an interest of your own. It will be a lifelong interest, and gradually it will fill your days. As Capricorn is the sign of worldly success, you will become a respected person in your field. How you go about this, and the manner in which it unfolds in your life, will depend on the houses (areas of life) your south and north nodes are in.

As with all south/north node positions, this will be a gradual process throughout the course of your life, and there is no need to take any conscious action. Life will present the opportunities for change. But one day, probably in older age, you will wake up and realize that you are on your way to worldly success, and while you still love your family as deeply as you ever did, you'll find it releasing not to have to be there for their every drama. You will have the space and time to find your own place in the world, to be known for something beyond your capacity for love. However, you won't be expected to stop looking after others entirely—when it comes to Capricorn, the help is financial. You can still help those you love, just in a different manner.

SOUTH NODE LEO ➡ NORTH NODE AQUARIUS

Leo Traits: *Loyal; warm; leader; talented; desires admiration*
Aquarius Traits: *Detached; impersonal; unemotional; objective; friendship more important than passionate love*

YOUR LAST LIFE: LEO SOUTH NODE

Leo is a very personal sign. It is a fire sign in the bottom half of the chart and is focused on outwardly expressing itself. Therefore, you come into this life with a knowledge of how to use your own talents to gain the respect and admiration of others. No matter what you actually do in life, you will be an actor, always seeking centre stage—often instinctively—which draws people into your sphere. You are great company and a warm and loyal friend. In your relationships, you are protective of those who adore you. In return, you need to feel appreciated and will expend any amount of effort on those who show how much they care. You need an outward expression of their love, so words are important. Like that actor onstage, when you do something of note, you need to hear applause or a word of thanks. Being appreciated pushes you to greater heights.

You come into this life with these traits as an innate part of who you are. You revel in being centre stage and are never shy of public speaking, acting, or singing in front of an appreciative audience. You are a warm and loving partner, full of charisma and style. Because of your need to stand out, you enjoy the best things in life, and you love mixing with the rich and famous; even better, you love being one of the beautiful people yourself. But the reality is, you don't mind who you mix with as long as they admire you.

THIS LIFETIME: AQUARIUS NORTH NODE

In this life, though, you will go through quite profound changes in your attitude, because Aquarius is the opposite of Leo in every sense. Where Leo is affectionate, Aquarius is detached. Aquarius views life objectively, moved only by curiosity and friendship, and isn't interested in the close mixing with people that occurred as a Leo. Leos love being in love, so they are prone to brief relationships, but Aquarius doesn't need close relationships. Being an air sign, they prefer to think rather than act, so they may analyse people and situations rather than personally partake in them.

Because Leo is the sign of royalty, you bring with you into this life the feeling of being special, and you still require that adoring audience. In the last life, you were definitely centre-stage in a leadership role that gained the attention and admiration of others. It is hard to change this innate feeling that you are special, that others are ordinary while you are not. It will be tempting to mix with people who stroke your ego.

But Aquarius is a personally cool, humanitarian sign that views everyone as equals, so as you go through life, in many gradual shifts and changes, you will lose your sense of specialness and come to see yourself differently. You will want to start using your personal talents for the betterment of all rather than for yourself alone. By the end of your life, doing something just for you will feel hollow; it will have to be accompanied by a more charitable purpose to feel of any value to you. Thus, you will lose your need for praise and do good deeds simply because you can use your talents in this way. Your satisfaction will come from within, rather than from outward praise. Your previous life of only mixing with people who told you how great you were will be replaced by a desire to mix with people who have the greater-good mindset.

In real terms, this could be using your talents for charitable organisations, helping those less fortunate, or being a spokesperson for a good cause; there are many and various ways this can pan out in life, and it will depend on the houses (areas of life) that are involved. But one way or another, by the end of your life, you will have learnt your life lesson of using your immense talents for the good of the whole and not just for self-promotion.

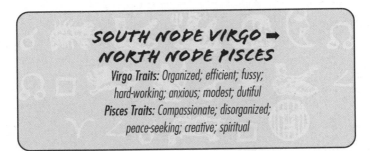

SOUTH NODE VIRGO ➡ NORTH NODE PISCES

Virgo Traits: *Organized; efficient; fussy; hard-working; anxious; modest; dutiful*

Pisces Traits: *Compassionate; disorganized; peace-seeking; creative; spiritual*

YOUR LAST LIFE: VIRGO SOUTH NODE

With your south node in Virgo, you came into this life with an eye for detail. From an early age you will notice when things aren't tidy and organized. You cannot live in chaos, so you soon start tidying away your toys. If mum or dad put you in mismatched socks, something you wore the day before, or even a jumper with a stain, it really bothered you all day. Fast forward to adulthood and this trait will be fully formed. You see jobs to do everywhere you turn, and being dutiful and hardworking, you do them. Other people might be willing, but you know you do it best. You never shirk a job or a duty, so you will begin working as soon as you are old enough.

This is the mindset you brought into this life, this need to bring order out of chaos, but of course the universe isn't a place of order. People are untidy, often disorganized, and there are germs everywhere. You'd ideally take a huge box of antiseptic wipes with you and wipe down every person and surface you come in contact with so you don't catch anything.

This is an extreme example, but the sign of Virgo rules health in addition to detail and order. Virgos are often self-absorbed when it comes to their health and can stick to any regime they choose if they feel it will stave off illness. You see illness as just another thing that can't be easily controlled, and because you spent your last life trying to control everything, you still feel this compulsive need to make sure everything and everyone is neat and tidy and organized. Virgo is a logical sign ruled by Mercury, so details are the bane of your existence, but they are also your sense of joy.

THIS LIFETIME: PISCES NORTH NODE

It won't be easy for you to learn to let go in this life, but that is your life lesson. Your north node is in Pisces, the exact opposite mindset. Pisces is disorganized, fluid, imaginative, and not in the least logical. And Pisces offers universal love.

As your life progresses, you will come to see how critical you are via small shifts and changes. You will realize that trying to bring order and create boundaries is exhausting and never really works because the job is too vast; it's an impossible task. Despite all your efforts, people go their own way. The constant work of trying to organize everything, to control it in effect, brings on bouts of nervousness, irritability, and maybe even a breakdown. When this happens, you will be forced to let go of the need to control yourself, those around you, and your environment.

This position of the nodes is asking you to figuratively jump into the abyss, to learn to go with the flow rather than trying to organize it. To do this requires you to become less logical and more intuitive, less of a thinking person and more of a feeling person. Pisces is a water sign, so it is sensitive and compassionate. It judges no one and accepts life as it flows around them. Doing nothing but tuning in, they resonate to higher energies and absorb nuances beyond the visible.

It will be hard to stop trying to control everything and everyone, and to ignore the chaos you naturally see. The fear that something is out there waiting to take you down the moment you allow a surface to remain unwiped, or a cup unwashed, needs to be shed. It really doesn't matter in the grand scheme of things if ornaments are not evenly placed or if there is a pile of newspapers on a surface.

In order to tap into some Pisces energy, you could train as a healer or a counsellor. Your path in this life is to learn to be less critical and more accepting. As a Pisces, you will learn that nothing can be controlled, neither people, the chaos in the world, the illnesses we are prone to, nor the structures we create. In reality, we are hurtling through space on a rock, so nothing about our world is safe nor predictable. Your lesson in this life is to close your eyes and take a leap of faith into the waters of Pisces, to accept that there is a reason and a purpose far greater than any of us can see, and to trust in a higher force. One way or another, life will present opportunities for you to move from Virgo to Pisces so that by the end of your life, you will be more relaxed, less fussy, and more loving.

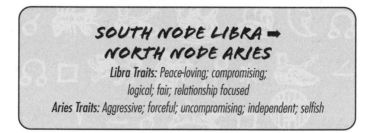

SOUTH NODE LIBRA ➡ NORTH NODE ARIES

Libra Traits: *Peace-loving; compromising; logical; fair; relationship focused*
Aries Traits: *Aggressive; forceful; uncompromising; independent; selfish*

YOUR LAST LIFE: LIBRA SOUTH NODE

Like all of the nodal positions, Aries and Libra are opposites. Libra is the sign of compromise and harmony. You come into this life as a people-pleaser. If others are happy, you are happy, and you detest confrontation and arguments; you make a quick exit when people become aggressive because it upsets your delicate balance.

Libra's symbol is the scales, which shows your desire to listen to everyone's point of view and then weigh that against your own desires. You'll find a middle road that placates everyone. Libra rules partnerships for this very reason, because living with someone in harmony is a delicate balancing act between pleasing them and being yourself; you both need to be able to express who you are, and your sign is the epitome of the perfect balance that results in harmony.

Because of this past-life pattern, you tend to get walked over. Not necessarily in a horrible way, but with your desire to please being so evident, strong, forceful types may ride roughshod over you. It's hard for you to think of yourself as an individual. In the last life, you were in one or more long-term relationships and learned how to compromise, and now you find it impossible to come to a decision if it involves denying another person their wishes, to the detriment of yourself. Being fair all the time seems to put you in a position where everyone else gets what they want, but you don't. Your lesson in this life is that you can't please all of the people all of the time, no matter how much you wish you could.

THIS LIFETIME: ARIES NORTH NODE

The north node in Aries shows your direction, and as you can see, the sign of Aries is pretty tough! It's a sign with a "me first" attitude in its rawest form. But how do you go about it moving from Libra to Aries? How do you suddenly become someone who does as they please?

Firstly, be aware that you do not have to take any conscious action. Life will present opportunities and circumstances for you to gradually move from Libra to Aries without much thought. It tends to be a natural progression throughout life, but it's helpful to be open to change, and to accept opportunities when they present themselves.

Your life's aim is to become less balanced and logical—Libra is an air sign, so you've been used to thinking about decisions—and more instinctive, which is an Aries trait. Aries see something, they want it, so they go get it, regardless of what other people want or think. They don't care what others think.

This will sound a bit harsh to someone so kind, but you do need to learn to stand up for yourself. To do this requires you to act a bit quicker, because the longer you hesitate, the more time you have time to think about an action, and being the person you are, you will naturally take others into account. Look at it from another angle.

You've already spent one or more lifetimes learning how to compromise. It is time for you to learn to be more independent and forceful about what you want. Isn't it about time that *you* were pleased for a change?

Any time in life that you are pushed to make a choice, try to do it as quickly as possible, and base it on your gut feeling. That's what Aries does. It's a fire sign, which thinks and acts very quickly. Fire signs are intuitive, so their instinctive feeling is the one they follow. In this life you are learning how to trust your gut—your very first instinct about anything and everything. Never mind what others will think; they'll be okay with whatever you choose because we all admire boldness, so long as it is accompanied by friendliness and good cheer, and this comes easily to an Aries. By the time you are at the end of your life, you will naturally accept being in charge and will easily bear the weight of responsibility that comes with decision-making.

Your Libra south node has made you passive, indecisive, and desirous of a harmonious partnership, but Aries will teach you boldness, bravery, and independence. You may just find you really enjoy doing what you want for a change—there is a freedom in it that you revel in.

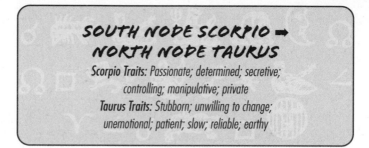

SOUTH NODE SCORPIO →
NORTH NODE TAURUS

Scorpio Traits: *Passionate; determined; secretive;*
controlling; manipulative; private
Taurus Traits: *Stubborn; unwilling to change;*
unemotional; patient; slow; reliable; earthy

YOUR LAST LIFE: SCORPIO SOUTH NODE

Scorpio is a deeply emotional and passionate sign. That's because it is a fixed water sign, and water represents emotion. Fixed water, though? How do you fix water? You build a wall around it, like a well. Then those emotions become deeper and darker. These are the energies Scorpio works with.

You came into this life understanding this all too well. Passion is often only thought of in connection with sex, but you feel deeply passionate about everything. Anything you do in life is pursued with a steely determination to understand everything, to dig deep and find any secrets. This applies to people, too, which is why Scorpio has such a bad reputation. You spend a lot of time analysing partners to see what makes them tick. Sometimes it is in order to control them; sometimes to find out if they have a secret agenda; sometimes in order to know what makes them happy—it depends on how highly evolved you are.

Scorpios can reach the heights of spiritual awakening, but they can also revel in the lower passions.

The lower level of the Scorpio mind revels in power games, mental manipulation, and the control of others. Those who are not spiritually developed may want to get revenge for real or imagined wrongs. They will enjoy creating dramatic situations and can destroy a really good relationship because of their desire to stir up things. They enjoy creating chaos and then blaming the result on others, of living a life of high drama, so they consciously rock the boat when things get dull.

The reality is, you are vulnerable to being hurt; all water signs are sensitive. This drama, secrecy, and investigation are your attempt to prevent being hurt. Everything you do is for self-protection.

THIS LIFETIME: TAURUS NORTH NODE

The hardest thing for you in this life will be to let go of the suspicion that everyone is out to mislead you. As you move towards the calm, unemotional, and patient sign of Taurus, the desire to dig deep will fade. Somehow, it won't matter anymore. In truth, those passionate emotions are tiring—exhausting, in fact—especially as life progresses. You will long to be at peace, and you will consciously choose to not overreact.

It could be that age brings physical infirmity, which means an overreaction will be detrimental to your health.

These dramas will take a toll on your mind and body. Or, this shift may come earlier, when you find yourself in a situation that requires a more measured, calm approach. Whatever way they present themselves, situations will appear throughout your life that require you to subdue the emotional turmoil inside of you and to accept that people are not out to deceive you, that they are genuine. Gradually, you will learn to see the best in people rather than the worst.

Scorpio is a taker. It drains people; it asks much of them. It is rarely a generous sign, unless there is some personal reward at the end of it. On the other hand, Taurus is a giver. It provides material security. Thus, there will be a shift in the way you treat people as life goes on. You will learn to accept others as they are, believe them when they talk, and provide for them. Your suspicious nature will subside, and the calm serenity that comes with Taurus will be balm to your ravaged soul. All that drama is put aside. Now and again it may surface, but you will learn to let drama go; it really is too much trouble and causes too much fallout.

Find a way of expressing your emotions that does not involve people; take up art, or writing, or learn to play a musical instrument. You will end your life quietly, living in peace and harmony, and you will learn to find joy in the simple pleasures: a sunset, a walk along the shore, or the wind in the trees. Nature will restore you.

SOUTH NODE SAGITTARIUS ➡ NORTH NODE GEMINI

Sagittarius Traits: *Friendly; intellectual; truthful; seeking*
Gemini Traits: *Communicative; gossipy; unreliable; changeable; fun; humorous*

YOUR LAST LIFE: SAGITTARIUS SOUTH NODE

At first glance, the traits for Sagittarius and Gemini don't seem that different, do they? And they are pretty similar in many ways. But Sagittarius is a fire sign and Gemini is an air sign, so their motivations are different. Plus, one is at the bottom of the chart, and one is at the top.

Sagittarius and Gemini both use communication in their lives, but in different ways. Sagittarius rules the ninth house of esoteric wisdom. Signs at the top of the chart are more detached and reasoning. Sagittarius analyses what people say and thinks about the philosophy of life. When this is your south node, you are highly intelligent and resonate with esoteric ideas, so you find it hard to fit in with ordinary people, who appear (to be honest) not very bright and certainly not on your wavelength.

This is because in the last life you probably spent a lot of time in private study. You would have enjoyed meeting people, but only to analyse their beliefs and ideas. From all of these threads you collected throughout your life, you stitched a meaning and purpose of life that resonated with you. It's unlikely you ever took people at face value or believed their words just because they appeared to have authority. You listened, but you sifted the information; some ideas you could accept, while others you would have discarded.

This is because Sagittarius is the sign of the truth-seeker. To be this way often requires freedom of movement. You may have travelled in search of ancient remains, worked as a travel writer or artist, taught at revered universities, or become an expert in an obscure field. In whatever way you expressed your Sagittarian need to explore, learn, and teach, it's likely you either had no long-term relationship or a very tolerant partner. Your mind focused on ideas, not relationships.

So, you came into this life with this mindset. You find it hard to fit in with normal life—it doesn't feel right. The people around you do not think as deeply as you do; they blindly accept their lot. You will find yourself being very critical of those not on your wavelength. You also find it hard to adhere to the customs and rules of society because of your far-seeing intellect. You don't want to be part of a group because you have nothing to say to them, and nothing they say to you is important enough to hold your attention. Sometimes you'll feel you come from a different planet altogether!

At first you are not sure why you have trouble accepting the restraints of society, but enlightenment gradually dawns. Until then, you are critical of those less clever and tend to keep to yourself—unless you meet someone of like mind, when the ideas will cascade out of you like a waterfall. At last, a kindred spirit!

THIS LIFETIME: GEMINI NORTH NODE

The sign of Gemini rules the third house of communication. It is down in the collective, the bottom of the chart. Having come from the top of the chart, the thinking area, the last thing you want to do is to mix with everyone, to live cheek by jowl with those you have nothing to say to, and to accept all the rules and regulations of society that accompany life when one is in a group setting.

As with all the nodal positions, moving from one sign to another—in your case, Sagittarius to Gemini—will be a gradual process throughout your life. As time goes on, there will be shifts and changes in the way you think, in the way you observe things, and in the way you express your ideas.

There is no point repeating a past-life pattern simply because it feels comfortable and familiar. Now, in this life, you will be asked to pass on the knowledge you learned in the last life to the collective as a teacher or educator. It can be in any field, from engineering to philosophy; your skill will be great in whatever field you are knowledgeable, and the world needs this. You are not meant to keep your knowledge to yourself.

Gradually, you will find a way of relating to others on a more basic level. After all, a teacher needs to be able to explain a subject, so the way you communicate, and your attitude towards those you teach, will alter. You will see we are all on our own pathway—some higher, some lower— and all are valid. The wisdom you acquired and brought with you has to be shared. It is no good keeping it for yourself alone.

When living and mixing with people in the collective, you have to conform to their rules, so very gradually you will begin to accept the restraints society imposes. You will see these customs serve a purpose of allowing us to live together in peace, with a structure that has formed over the entire lifetime of the human race for just this purpose. If everyone felt as you did, anarchy would reign.

In order to function in the collective and be accepted as a teacher, you will be required to think about things like your appearance and behaviour. You'll learn how to be polite to people, even when they are not on your wavelength, and how to effectively communicate profound ideas at a level that can be understood. Eventually you will come to see that we are all in mutually beneficial relationships, that we rely on each other, and that we all have our place. In the end, you will see that it is okay to be normal and to enjoy life with those you may once have considered your intellectual inferiors.

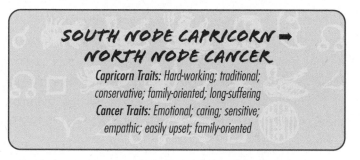

SOUTH NODE CAPRICORN ➡ NORTH NODE CANCER

Capricorn Traits: Hard-working; traditional; conservative; family-oriented; long-suffering

Cancer Traits: Emotional; caring; sensitive; empathic; easily upset; family-oriented

YOUR LAST LIFE: CAPRICORN SOUTH NODE

When your south node is in Capricorn, you are naturally responsible. People sense this capable attitude and place you in positions of authority. Therefore, you will have no trouble acquiring the respect of your peers and an impressive position in your career—you may even have a meteoric rise to the top of the career ladder. You radiate tradition, reliability, an innate sense of duty, and a good work ethic. It is likely, then, that life will present no problems in the field of work, and the concomitant financial rewards will fall into your lap.

With this south node sign, even if you discover early in life that your path is different, others will think of you as a Capricorn and suggest careers and opportunities. So strong is this sign that it will be hard for others to see you in a less-than-exalted position, and some may even berate you for your lack of drive and social status if you resist the opportunities presented.

Let's assume you head out into the world and get started on your career. As soon as your school years are behind you, your innate confidence opens doors. It won't be long before you are assuming a high-profile role, as you did in the last life. It is easy for you to lead and control, to be in charge of people. It takes no effort for you to know the right way to go about business, and your people skills are pretty good too.

But by doing this, you are repeating a past-life pattern. It's second nature to you because you've done it all before, but life is a learning process, so repeating patterns is pointless. The problem with the sign of Capricorn is that everyone else senses it too, so they continue to push you into that past-life pattern.

THIS LIFETIME: CANCER NORTH NODE

Capricorn's opposite sign is Cancer, and this is the sign you will be heading towards in this life. When you read over Cancerian traits, you will feel a sense of deflation. Caring? Sensitive? Emotional? You won't relate to any of these because you are intelligent, logical, earthy, and driven. But as life goes by, you will slowly become more like Cancer and less career-focused. There are many and various ways this could pan out. Perhaps you find a family member needs you and there is no one else who can assume the role of carer; maybe your career unexpectedly takes a nose dive; maybe your skillset is no longer required in the world; maybe your partner is offered a once-in-a-lifetime opportunity and needs you to be supportive.

How the changes occur will depend very much on the rest of your chart and the house (area of life) the north node is in. But the result is you will be forced to stay home for a while, assuming the chores and tasks of the household: cooking, cleaning, shopping, dealing with children, looking after someone who is elderly or ill, etc. This will be hard because caring is very often a thankless task, and you are accustomed to being respected and admired. Because caring is never-ending, thanks wane after a while; people take their carer for granted. Indeed, they may adore you for what you do, but continual thanks end up sounding meaningless. So, you will find yourself looking after people just because you can and without any thought of praise. Your high-profile career disappears and you are left with those you love, but you will come to realize their opinions matter far more.

There are many ways of showing a caring nature. You could become a counsellor or a healer; caring takes many forms, but as long as you are using your skills with people in a caring manner, you will be on the right path.

Both these signs are family-minded, but Capricorn wants to help the family financially, to get their children into good schools and to provide for them. Cancer, on the other hand, offers more emotional support; it has an empathic side that Capricorn doesn't. Capricorn is at the top of the chart, where it stands out from the crowd, but Cancer is down in the bottom; it rules the fourth house. The fourth house is our roots, the family we sprang from, and the family we go on to create. It is not visible to the world because when we close our door, we close out the world; it is our family who know and love us best.

Becoming more like a Cancerian means becoming more humble. It means taking your place in a unit, whether that is your own family or the family of humankind. Many Cancerians offer care to those in their community: often they choose to be carers, nurses, paramedics, doctors, healers, or counsellors. It means relinquishing the need to control, the desire to stand out from the crowd, and the aspiration of worldly status and rewards. It means not falling into the trap of working yourself into a state of martyrdom to gain recognition and status, which will never come with a Cancer north node.

It's hard, but you have to let the world go by without taking part. Deal with the needs of those closest to you, learn how to love in an emotional way rather than a practical way, be part of a team, listen, adapt, and give. Expect no reward except the love of those you care for.

SOUTH NODE AQUARIUS → NORTH NODE LEO

Aquarius Traits: Detached; non-judgemental; unemotional; humanitarian; quirky
Leo Traits: Loyal; proud; self-expressive; seeks praise and admiration

YOUR LAST LIFE: AQUARIUS SOUTH NODE

Aquarius is a detached, cool, air sign ruled by Uranus, an unpredictable planet. This makes you a law unto yourself, which you love. No one can tie you down, contain you, or suppress your individuality. You are original and unique, and you see life objectively. Your ego is probably non-existent, and you are not materialistic in the least. You find the way that people strive and jostle for positions of power—and for love—to be curious; you never allow yourself to get personally involved or drawn into the melee of life.

This sign has many friendships, and that is the best you can do: friendship. Personal relationships are hard for someone who doesn't understand emotions and who prefers the drama in their life to come from scientific breakthroughs, not their partner losing it. Aquarians do form partnerships sometimes, but you are never totally attached to anyone or anything. You probably partner up because everyone else is doing it, and you want to know what all the fuss is about. To be honest, you could take or leave most things in life, including love. As for passion, the word is not in your vocabulary. You enjoy using logic, and your best trait is your ability to see the ridiculousness of the human condition; you either laugh at life yourself or make other people laugh by drawing attention to the absurdities.

Aquarius rules the eleventh house. At the highest level, this is the place where leaders in their chosen field make decisions on behalf of others; think the House of Lords in England or the Senate in America. To do this requires a detached, intellectual logic used to benefit mankind, and this is the highest expression of the sign of Aquarius. Even those who don't reach these heady heights will choose friendship over love and be detached and cool in all human interactions.

THIS LIFETIME: LEO NORTH NODE

On the other hand, Leo is a personal sign. Leo rules the fifth house, which is at the bottom of the chart. All of the houses at the bottom of the chart are personal. This area of life is concerned with self-expression. The best description of Leo is as an actor; Leo develops their own personal talents in order to be noticed. They want to stand centre stage, where they can be admired and praised.

You can see how different these two signs are. However, there is a meeting point: both signs enjoy serving others. Leo, at its core, serves others in a blaze of publicity, but nevertheless, they thrive on doing something worthwhile. They seek to command and can assume responsibility. The more they are praised, the more they strive to do. Being a spokesperson for a charity, organizing events that help others, or even getting on stage to raise money for a worthy cause—they enjoy all of these things because the more they do in charitable terms, the more highly others think of them.

In this life, opportunities will be presented to you that allow you to become less Aquarian and more Leo-like. You will be asked to stand centre stage. You won't necessarily want to, but you won't baulk at the idea either. While Aquarians are reluctant to stand up and be counted because it pins them down to a commitment, they have the social skills necessary to get it done.

Becoming more Leo-like means living down at the bottom of the chart rather than at the top. You pride yourself on being detached, but Leo is not a detached sign. The fifth house is an area of human activity; it's the bar, the pub, the theatre, a busy restaurant, or the club. This means you are being asked to mix with all sorts of people from all walks of life. Connect with people in a tactile way, build relationships (they are often brief in this house), and mix with all and sundry. You can mix with anyone, but your main difficulty will be learning to express yourself in a personal way.

There will always be a desire to return to the area you find comfortable, but Aquarian characteristics will be a step backwards in your soul development. You've always dealt with everything in life quietly and unassumingly, but now you are being asked to do it in a blaze of glory. You will have to stop daydreaming and start acting. Learn to overcome any innate shyness. Take any leadership position you are offered, and accept that you do have the tools to lead, and also the charisma. Use your humour to cajole your audience. Even though you believe in potential, the fact of the matter is that some people are better at leading than others.

You are being asked to bring your love of humanity to the fore, and to use your skills to capture the attention of the world. This will lead to success, admiration, and praise, but also to something far more valuable: inner satisfaction and joy.

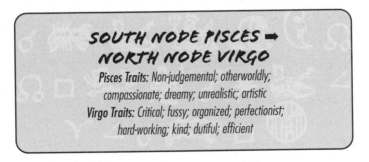

SOUTH NODE PISCES → NORTH NODE VIRGO

Pisces Traits: Non-judgemental; otherworldly; compassionate; dreamy; unrealistic; artistic

Virgo Traits: Critical; fussy; organized; perfectionist; hard-working; kind; dutiful; efficient

YOUR LAST LIFE: PISCES SOUTH NODE

You came into this life with an innate compassion and understanding of your fellow man. Pisces is a mutable water sign, so you see everything as part of a wider, universal whole. Because of this, you have unending love for your fellow humans, regardless of status. You see beyond the trappings of the material world to people's inner being, and you see that we are all souls striving towards enlightenment. Thus, who are you to judge anyone?

Every single person's pain and suffering affects you deeply. So deeply, in fact, that you avoid becoming embroiled. It is not that you don't care (you most certainly do), but you do not have the tools to do anything but understand, offer a few words of love, and move on. Your feelings run so deep that you risk being overwhelmed by the pain and loss in the world, and many Pisceans cope with drugs or alcohol in the face of so much unhappiness. Other Pisceans express their feelings through art or music, follow a religion that resonates with them, or retreat into illness, either real or imagined. Life is a hard place for as sensitive a soul as yours.

But remember, that was your last life. You came into this life still carrying this capacity to be long-suffering, to understand and sympathize with others, and to follow your instincts, on which you rely so much. But the world is a confusing place for such a tender, instinctual being, and you lack confidence. You also suffer from inner confusion, which makes you appear befuddled and disorganized, and therefore easy prey for those who wish to rule or control you.

The trouble is, people tend to latch on to you because you are so kind and have such strong compassion. Your friendly nature means you find it hard to say no, which draws the weakest and most needy people into your sphere.

THIS LIFETIME: VIRGO NORTH NODE

The characteristics of Virgo will seem alien. Organized? Efficient? It is not that you don't want to be, but you haven't the slightest idea how to go about it! You live in a bit of a muddle because you rely on your gut instincts. (Invariably, your gut instincts are right, but that won't help you much in our dog-eat-dog-world.) Take it slow. Let life guide you towards Virgo in small steps and changes. Change doesn't happen overnight, but over a whole lifetime. You don't even have to consciously do anything except be open to opportunities to become more like a Virgo.

Virgo is the sign you will resonate with by the end of your life. It still serves others, but it does so more practically. Virgo organizes and plans. You could start embodying Virgo energy by making lists, then working your way through them. Virgo also works hard; it rules the sixth house of hands-on physical labour. So, if details are anathema to you, why not try some physical work? This nodal position is saying you have to stop daydreaming and start taking action.

It will be so tempting to retreat back to your dreamy world, where you try to look after everyone who asks for your help, but you have to avoid falling into that trap this time. Do not overlook unacceptable behaviour. You make excuses for everyone, and now this must stop. People will always try to manipulate your good nature, so when you notice it happening, you must resist being swayed. You have to learn to say no. It needn't be unkindly said, but it must be firm. You will be required throughout your life to be more logical and organized, and one of the first steps is knowing where to draw the line when people overstep the mark.

Both of these signs serve others, but while a Pisces south node served everyone without discrimination, now you must serve only those who really need it, and you must let those who lean on you stand on their own two feet. This will require you to have a strong mind and a greater determination, but as life progresses, you will find the inner strength to slough off those who drain you so that you can focus on those who truly need you.

four
Combining the Nodes and the Signs

In order to show you how the nodes and the signs work together, here are two examples.

EXAMPLE: SOUTH NODE IN CANCER IN THE NINTH HOUSE ➡ NORTH NODE IN CAPRICORN IN THE THIRD HOUSE

When the south node is in the ninth house and the north node is in the third, communication and thought are going to be the focus of your life lessons, because these two houses are on the thinking axis.

The south node in the ninth house suggests you spent your last lifetime in study, and you formed your own views about life. But in this life, you will be asked to try and communicate those ideas to the general public—the collective—in a way they can understand.

Because the south node is a comfort area, you won't want to do this; you will long to be left alone so you can continue your studies and research. However, as you go through life, various opportunities will present themselves to you that might encourage you to teach what you know, or to communicate it via writing, singing, or acting. (Any form of communication is fine.)

As the third house rules the local community, you may be forced to live in the collective even though you would rather be isolated from people. Perhaps your life circumstances mean you cannot afford to remove yourself to a more remote location, or perhaps you rely on people to help you. In one way or another, you will certainly have some contact with this third-house area during your life, but there will always be a desire to be back in your ivory tower, left alone to indulge in private study. If it were up to you, you would live in a remote area and be selectively social.

So, how do you have to express yourself in this third house? This is where the astrological signs of your nodes provide greater detail.

With the south node in Cancer and the north node in Capricorn, this suggests that your last life was spent being a carer. Regardless of your past-life sun sign, your south node in Cancer would have placed you in a position where you were required to look after others in some way. Perhaps you looked after someone in particular, like a family member. Maybe you did live in a remote area so you had to rely on your own resources rather than seeking the company of friends and neighbours. Either way, your position enabled you to have quiet time in which to think about things and to develop your own philosophy about life without the influence of others to sway you.

With Cancer as your south node sign, you will still feel the desire to take care of people, especially family members, and it will be quite natural for you to assume the role of carer. It is something you do comfortably, and well. It's instinctual because you've had so much previous experience with it. You may start looking after others at a very young age.

But your north node is Capricorn in this life. It will take many years to reach your north node house. Capricorn is ruled by Saturn, which indicates that there will be blocks and obstacles along your path. That is the first thing to note. The next is that Capricorn rules the tenth house of career, so it will be via a career that you will reach your north node—but you won't want one. You are perfectly content being a carer and working in a hands-on way behind the scenes, while spending your spare time alone with your thoughts or enjoying private study. The last thing you want is to be at the top of the birth chart, being recognized in a high-profile career. It is the exact opposite of what makes you feel comfortable.

Your nodes are saying that slowly and surely, and in a gradual way, those you care for won't need you quite as much. While that is happening, you will also discover that there are people who want to hear what you have to say, so you might take up a bit of teaching or writing. This exploration may start in a very small way, such as teaching in your own home or at a small venue.

One way or another, and in small progressions, you will reach a point where you are no longer needed as a carer, and indeed, you may lose the desire to look after people as time goes on. Age tends to bring this anyway; people who have constantly cared for others grow weary as life progresses and prefer to leave this task to those with more youth and energy.

Life will present opportunities for you to teach what you know in one form or another. The sign of Capricorn indicates this will occur later in life, when wisdom and age have increased sufficiently. Nevertheless, you will find a willing audience for what you have to say. Thus, your previous life of private study will not be in vain.

There will be pleasure in being able to share your wisdom, but it is unlikely you will ever want to live among the collective. So, while there may be areas of joy, wholehearted fulfilment is unlikely, because your south node remains your comfort area throughout life. Always you will feel more "at home" living in an isolated manner and being left to your own devices. The exception is if you have an important planet in the same house as your north node, in which case there will be more of a drive to focus on this area, as well as more willingness to accept it. If you have planets in the south node house, this indicates there are still aspects of this area you have yet to fully integrate, so your life will be more of a balance of the two areas.

EXAMPLE: SOUTH NODE IN SCORPIO IN THE SEVENTH HOUSE ➡ NORTH NODE IN TAURUS IN THE FIRST HOUSE

Seventh/first house nodes show your life lessons will revolve around relationships; this is the relationship axis.

With the south node in the seventh house, you came into this life with the ability to form long-term partnerships easily. Because of your last life's experiences, you know exactly how to compromise and adapt to another person, and you prefer being in a twosome. This means you will want to hook up with someone pretty soon; as quickly as possible, typically. It may be that even as a child, you'd had a particularly close friend, and then, when older, a girlfriend or boyfriend, even by the age of seven or eight. Although this would technically not be considered a real partnership, this tendency shows your inner desire to be part of a couple.

Fast forward a few more years and you will be thinking of settling down. It is natural for you, it feels comfortable, and you'll have no trouble adapting and compromising to keep your partner happy. You won't be interested in brief liaisons; you seek a serious relationship. However, with your north node in the first house, your life challenge will be living alone.

It won't happen immediately, but life will present opportunities and experiences that steer you towards a single life. It will not be what you want, but you are learning how to be an individual, how to make decisions that concern you alone, and how to cope by yourself. Gradually, your mindset will alter, and by the time you are reaching old age, compromising will be more difficult. You'll want to think of yourself for a change! So, the move from one mindset to another will happen slowly over many years.

The sign in your seventh house is Scorpio. This will make you very passionate, with a need to focus on one person. Before committing to your long-term partner, you will have made sure they were genuine because you won't want to be hurt. Scorpio is ultra-sensitive, so you'll be cautious when it comes to giving your heart away. With that being said, your need for a partner drives you towards finding someone quite early on in life.

The sign of Scorpio makes you an intensely emotional person, and your loved one will have no doubt of your desire and love. But you might not be an easy partner to get along with. You may feel the need to constantly test them because of your desire to keep life exciting and dramatic. When life gets comfortable, you'll create a scene just to liven things up.

Taurus is the sign you are moving towards, and as time goes on, you will become calmer. All that intensity takes its toll on the body. Perhaps you will be advised to watch your blood pressure or live a quieter existence. Or maybe this change simply happens; you tire of drama and seek a more placid life. As that happens, you will find yourself living alone more. Perhaps that is why you become calmer, because you have no partner to stir up? Maybe your partner got tired of all the mind games and interplay—you'd have found that exciting, but maybe they didn't.

This is not to say you won't have a partner, but perhaps you will choose to live separately and only go out for meals and on holiday together. How this will pan out in life will depend on the rest of your chart and the choices you make. But one way or another, you will discover you can manage just fine on your own, and you will prefer a quiet life. Your inner turmoil will lessen. A peaceful older age is in store for you.

Conclusion

The rising sign has always perplexed me. We seem to innately use its characteristics from the moment of our birth, and I wondered why this is. This is especially unusual because there is not necessarily a planet in our rising sign, and nowhere else in the birth chart do we use an astrological sign that doesn't have a planet in it. I also questioned why we have a rising sign as a buffer between us and the rest of the world—why should one be necessary?

I was a student of the Huber school in the 1980s when I first learned of the nodes and their role in my life. This was a revelation. The fact that I resonated so strongly with my south node made me certain I'd found a real gem of wisdom that would help me live a more fulfilling life. In addition, I was taught that inhabiting my north node area of life would bring happiness and contentment. However, despite what I was taught, I've never felt particularly drawn to my north node area, not even with the passing years. When I began checking with clients and students, they felt similarly. It was helpful and enlightening to know what our intended path was, but it wasn't a place any of us wanted to go.

I've spent my whole adult life interpreting charts, and it is that wisdom, garnered over so many years with so many clients and students, that I used to form the ideas presented in this book. Over time, I realized that our rising sign has a deeper significance than previously thought, and I also discovered that we all gradually adopt *one area* of our north node house that is meaningful to us, but that this usually happens later in life. The people I've since interpreted charts for have felt likewise: their south and north node information helped them make sense of things and gave them a focus, a purpose to aim for.

Like many new theories, my insights came as a eureka moment, and the more I analysed them, the surer I felt. They made perfect sense in every way. Enlightenment comes to us in many ways, and bit by bit, we progress on the path to knowledge. I hope you have found this new interpretation of the rising sign and the nodes as fulfilling and life-affirming as I have.

Hopefully the insights offered in this book will contribute to your efforts to discover yourself and your life path using your birth chart, and will assist you in your own individual spiritual development.

Appendix
Astrology Basics

An astrological chart is a picture of the sky the moment we took our first breath. It shows the exact planetary placements we were born under. A birth chart is a circle with you at the centre. Imagine looking up from that centre, and this is the alignment of the astrological signs, planets, and houses at your moment of birth.

As the sky looks different from moment to moment and place to place, it is important to know the exact time and place of birth when calculating a birth chart. It's easy to see your birth chart; just go to any site that offers a free chart, type in your time, date, and place of birth, and print it out or take a screenshot.

Everything that you see in a birth chart means something about who you are and how you act, but it also covers important information about your destiny and life purpose. The easiest way of describing a birth chart is to say that it is a map of your life.

HOW DOES ASTROLOGY WORK?

A chart looks complicated when you first see it, but think of it like an onion, with each layer meaning something. Firstly, ancient astrologers divided the sky into the twelve astrological signs of Aries, Taurus, Gemini, Cancer, Leo, Virgo, Libra, Scorpio, Sagittarius, Capricorn, Aquarius, and Pisces based on the constellations. These are the symbols that go around the whole chart circle, and it's likely you recognize some (or most) of them.

The next thing you see in a birth chart are the planets, the ten astrological planets that are in fairly close proximity to Earth. They are the sun, moon, Mercury, Venus, Mars, Jupiter, Saturn, Uranus, Neptune, and Pluto. It's likely some of the symbols for the planets are recognizable to you; the moon, in particular.

Each planet has its own unique purpose and energy. For example, the planet Mercury rules how you think, speak, and communicate. Because of this mapping of the sky, each planet will fall in one of the astrological signs, and whichever astrological sign Mercury is in at your moment of birth will tell an astrologer how you think and speak.

There is another symbol in the chart that looks a bit like a headset. These are the north nodes, and they are your marker to this life's purpose.

But it doesn't stop there! Ancient astrologers also divided the sky into twelve houses, which are areas of life. (Descriptions of each are listed in the following pages.) The houses cover every aspect of human life. So, Mercury will be in an astrological sign, but it will also be in a *house*, and this will show an astrologer what area of life you think and speak about most.

The houses are not easy to see, but are usually shown by small lines coming out from the astrological signs. Usually they are black, but sometimes four important lines are marked in red: on the far left, the rising sign (still written as AC because it was previously referred to as the *ascendant*); at the bottom, the IC (a Latin phrase, *Imum Coeli*, which means "bottom of the sky"); the DC on the far right, which stands for the *descendant* and highlights the ways we interact with other people; and at the top, the MC, the *midheaven*, which is the highest point we can achieve in life, usually via our career.

The colourful lines you see spanning the chart are aspect lines and indicate links between planetary energies; they indicate if the planets are working in harmony or if their energies are in opposition, causing tension. The balance of coloured lines is also important; is one colour more dominant than the others?

Interpreting a chart involves analysing and assessing all this information: astrological sign characteristics, planet energies, houses, and aspect lines.

THE ZODIAC SIGNS

Each of the twelve zodiac signs has a unique energy and motivation. The easiest way to understand yours is through its element (fire, earth, air, or water) and its motivation (cardinal, fixed, or mutable). Knowing these two aspects will give you a really good idea of how a sign works.

ELEMENTS

- **Fire signs** are bold, adventurous, impatient, and driven.
- **Earth signs** are stable, seek security, and prefer the status quo.
- **Air signs** use their minds. Their motivation is to communicate, study, research, and teach.
- **Water signs** are the feeling signs. They are sensitive, empathic, and caring.

MOTIVATIONS

- **Cardinal signs** are capable, bold, and driven. They can pick themselves up after disasters.
- **Fixed signs** are stable, reliable, and stubborn. They dislike change, and they have difficulty adapting to new circumstances.
- **Mutable signs** are flexible and adaptable, so they handle life's fluctuations well, but they are hard to pin down.

SUN SIGNS

The sun is the most important planet in your birth chart, and the astrological sign it is in at your birth describes who you really are; it's how you express your identity and individuality.

The sun is the only planet that we can give dates to because it takes one year for the earth to circle the sun, unlike the other planets that move faster or slower and are difficult to assign exact dates to. Sometimes, though, even the sun's dates differ because the sky is a circle of 360 degrees, but there are 365 days in a year. This is why your time of birth needs to be accurate.

- **Aries** (March 21–April 19) is a cardinal fire sign. Aries suns are driven, capable, impatient and bold. They can cope with life's ups and downs and enjoy starting new things. Their symbol is the ram because they face life head-on and batter down opposition rather than avoid it.

- **Taurus** (April 20–May 20) is a fixed earth sign. Taurus suns are the most stable sign of the zodiac. They dislike change of any sort, and they stick with every choice they make, from their life partner to their house. They have trouble adapting to unexpected circumstances. Their symbol is the bull because of this fixity.

- **Gemini** (May 21–June 21) is a mutable air sign. Gemini is the most difficult sign to pin down. They thrive on communication, change, and variety, so they find it hard to stay put in one place, with one partner, or in one job. Their symbol is the twins, which shows their restless, changeable nature.

- **Cancer** (June 22–July 22) is a cardinal water sign. Cancer suns are sensitive and caring, but they are stronger than they look. Being a cardinal sign, they can cope with life's ups and downs. Their symbol is the crab, which shows how vulnerable they are, and how they protect themselves with a hard outer shell.

- **Leo** (July 23–August 22) is a fixed fire sign. They are warm, generous, and loyal, but they expect thanks for the considerable amount they do for others. This is shown by their symbol, the lion, who looks after their pride but expects to be number one.

- **Virgo** (August 23–September 22) is a mutable earth sign. Virgo suns are hard-working and dutiful but have high and exacting standards. Their symbol is the earth maiden who attends to the practical matters of life, which makes them really good with details.

- **Libra** (September 23–October 23) is a cardinal air sign. Libra suns are logical, balanced, and fair. The scales are their symbol, which shows how they use their minds to achieve harmony. They seek to keep everyone happy with their reasoned judgements.

- **Scorpio** (October 24–November 21) is a fixed water sign. Scorpio is famed for its passion and intensity. Water signs are deeply sensitive and emotional, and because of its fixity, Scorpio is unable to let slights go. Scorpio's symbol is the scorpion because they seek revenge on anyone who hurts them or their loved ones.

- **Sagittarius** (November 22–December 21) is a mutable fire sign, so Sagittarius suns are restless and changeable, forever on the move. Their symbol is the archer. Wherever the arrows land, Sagittarius will go in search of something new.

- **Capricorn** (December 22–January 19) is a cardinal earth sign. Capricorn suns focus on working hard and building security. They want to make their mark on the world, so they pursue money, real estate, and status. Their symbol is the goat, which shows their determination to reach the pinnacle of life, even if it is a slow ascent.

- **Aquarius** (January 20–February 18) is a fixed air sign. They are original and unpredictable, and their fixity shows in their determination to be themselves. They don't adapt to others—they go their own way. Their symbol is the water carrier, which reflects their humanitarian drive.

- **Pisces** (February 19–March 20) is a mutable water sign. Pisces suns are extremely sensitive and compassionate, but because they are mutable, they are impossible to pin down; they slip away to calm waters when life gets tough. Their symbol shows two fish swimming in opposite directions, which reflects their inability to make decisions.

Some people think they are "on the cusp" of two signs (and are a bit of both signs), but your time of birth will tell you which sign you really are. And, unless you have another planet in that other sign, you won't exhibit any of its traits, no matter how close your sun is to the actual start of the sign.

THE PLANETS

The ten astrological planets are the sun, moon, Mercury, Venus, Mars, Jupiter, Saturn, Uranus, Neptune, and Pluto. They each reflect different facets of our personality.

The first seven are called *personal planets* because these are used in everyday life. The three outer planets (Uranus, Neptune, and Pluto) are called *transpersonal planets*. They move very slowly across the sky, and therefore whole generations of people have them in the same sign (though not in the same house).

- **Sun:** The sun's position in the chart, by astrological sign and house, shows your main focus in life and where you get your sense of identity.
- **Moon:** The moon's position, by sign and house, shows how you respond emotionally.
- **Mercury:** This planet's position explains how you learn, teach, and communicate.
- **Venus:** The position of Venus shows how you love and what brings you contentment.
- **Mars:** The position of Mars, by sign and house, shows what drives you in life.

- **Jupiter:** Where Jupiter falls is an area of abundance and pleasure.
- **Saturn:** Traditionally, Saturn's sign and house show the difficulties you will face in life.
- **Uranus:** This planet shows the area of life where sudden, unexpected disruption is likely to occur.
- **Neptune:** Its position shows the area of life where confusion and deception will abound.
- **Pluto:** This planets reveals the area of life we want to control.

When the outer planets (Uranus, Neptune, and Pluto) are in conjunction with (right next to) other planets, especially the personal ones, they can radically affect them, making them more disruptive and unpredictable (Uranus), vague (Neptune), or controlling (Pluto).

The north node is not a planet, but a past-life marker. It shows us our cosmic path. Technically, it's a mathematical point relating to the positions of the sun, moon, and Earth at the moment of birth; it is the point at which the moon's orbit intersected the plane of the ecliptic.

THE HOUSES

Houses are areas of life. A birth chart is divided into twelve houses. When a planet falls in a particular house, its energies are interpreted in context of the meaning of the house.

The first house is the ascendant/rising sign and reflects how we appear to others or wish to be perceived. The houses go in sequence, starting with the rising sign, and move counterclockwise around the chart.

1. The rising sign and how you want others to see you
2. Money and possessions
3. Communication/education
4. Home and family
5. Creativity, fertility, and self-expression
6. Work, health, and service to others
7. Marriage and long-term partnerships
8. Sex, death, psychology, and what other people own
9. Travel, philosophy, and higher learning
10. Career and status
11. Friendships, groups, and shared ideals
12. The hidden self and spiritual beliefs

HOUSE RULERS

Each house relates to an astrological sign, which is called its ruler. They go in sequence, from Aries to Pisces, counterclockwise from the rising sign. So, the rising sign is ruled by Aries, the second house by Taurus, the third by Gemini, and so forth.

Very often, beginners get confused by this concept. But a ruler is just an easy way of remembering what the house is all about. For example, Gemini rules the third house, and therefore this house has a Gemini feel: it's about communication, friends, neighbours, and the local community. Planets here will want to express themselves in a Gemini way by teaching, communicating, and being active in the community, regardless of what astrological sign is in the third house in an individual's chart.

As an example, if a chart has the sign of Scorpio in the third house, the individual will approach teaching and learning in a Scorpio way: with intensity and purpose. And they will be reserved in the way they communicate. If Capricorn is in third, they will want to study traditional subjects or teach the way it's always been done, and they will express conservative views. Aquarius, on the other hand, will prefer unusual subjects; if a teacher, the individual will teach in a completely different way or find new ways of teaching. They will enjoy shocking people by expressing different and unusual views. Aries will be quick to learn, and not afraid of expressing their opinions. And so on.

ASPECTS

Aspects are links between planets. Very close aspects mean the planet energies work together. Aspects will show up as lines in a birth chart, and they will be various colours. Every site does the colours a bit differently, though I've shared here the standard colours used for these lines.

The main aspects are:

- **Conjunction:** Planets right next to, or within a few degrees of, each other. Sometimes the colour orange is used to show a conjunction.
- **Semi-Sextile:** A short line 30 degrees between planets that shows a natural and easy working between the planets involved. No effort is required; it is an innate ability. Often, this line is depicted as green.
- **Sextile:** An easy link between planets 60 degrees apart. Usually shown as a short blue line.
- **Square:** A short line 90 degrees between planets that shows an energetic, working energy between them. This line is typically red in a birth chart.
- **Trine:** An aspect 120 degrees apart between planets. This is drawn as a long blue line and reflects a harmonious link between the planets involved.
- **Quincunx:** A long green line 150 degrees between planets that shows a searching quality; very often,

there is a divine discontent with this—there is knowledge of something more but an inability to find it, which leads to a constant vague discontent.

- **Opposition:** A long line (often red) that spans the whole chart, 180 degrees apart. This line indicates a tension between two planets that is rarely resolved. In particular, when the sun and moon are in opposition, this can cause lifelong difficulties.

TO WRITE TO THE AUTHOR

If you wish to contact the author or would like more information about this book, please write to the author in care of Llewellyn Worldwide Ltd. and we will forward your request. Both the author and publisher appreciate hearing from you and learning of your enjoyment of this book and how it has helped you. Llewellyn Worldwide Ltd. cannot guarantee that every letter written to the author can be answered, but all will be forwarded. Please write to:

Andrea Taylor
℅ Llewellyn Worldwide
2143 Wooddale Drive
Woodbury, MN 55125-2989

Please enclose a self-addressed stamped envelope for reply,
or $1.00 to cover costs. If outside the U.S.A., enclose
an international postal reply coupon.

Many of Llewellyn's authors have websites with additional information and resources. For more information, please visit our website at http://www.llewellyn.com.

NOTES

NOTES

NOTES

NOTES

NOTES